NEW
DECORATOR

CREATIVE
HOME
ARTS
—CLUB—

CREATIVE HOME ARTS LIBRARY™

Ultimately, the greatest success of a house is that

NEW DECORATOR

JULIA BARNARD WITH NICHOLAS BARNARD

we can live comfortably and unselfconsciously.

CREATIVE
HOME
ARTS
—CLUB—

MINNETONKA, MINNESOTA

CREATIVE
HOME
ARTS
CLUB

A DK PUBLISHING BOOK

Senior Editor • Gillian Roberts
Project Art Editors • Wendy Bartlet, Clive Hayball
US Editor • Alrica Green
Picture Researcher • Mollie Gillard
DTP Designer • Matthew Greenfield
Senior Managing Editor • Mary-Clare Jerram
Managing Art Editor • Amanda Lunn
Commissioned Photography • James Merrell, Nick Pope
Production Controller • Wendy Penn
Cover Design, Text and Production • Julie Cisler,
Tom Carpenter, Michele Teigen

2 3 4 5 / 06 05 04 03 02

Published in the United States by DK Publishing, Inc.
375 Hudson Street, New York, New York 10014

This edition published for the Creative Home Arts Club
by Dorling Kindersley in 2002

Copyright © 1999, 2000 Dorling Kindersley Limited, London
Text copyright © 1999, 2000 Julia Barnard

A CIP record for this book is available from
the Library of Congress

ISBN 0-7894-8976-7

Text film output by R & B Creative Services
Reproduced in Singapore by Chroma Graphics
Printed and bound in China by Toppan

Contents

Introduction

WHETHER CHOOSING THE DECOR or considering improvements, it is important to remember that the word "home" describes not just a place or dwelling but also a state of being. Home embraces our fundamental need for domestic comfort, irrespective of fashion, philosophy, or time, but it is more than somewhere to lay your head. To a small child, home is the entire universe, and the first shelter of the imagination; for most of us, it is a calm haven in a hectic world. People everywhere have venerated their homes, honoring them as they would a god. While a building is first and foremost a composition of planes and angles, when animated by human experience it goes beyond mere geometry. As the French philosopher, Gaston Bachelard, wrote: *All really inhabited space bears the essence of the notion of home.*

When we choose furnishings and fabrics, wallpaper and paint, functional objects and decorative accessories to use and enjoy, we give life to our surroundings and so bring greater meaning to our lives. It is then that our home becomes a vital extension of who we are. It tells a story about us and how we see the world, and is expressive of our interests and beliefs even when we aren't there.

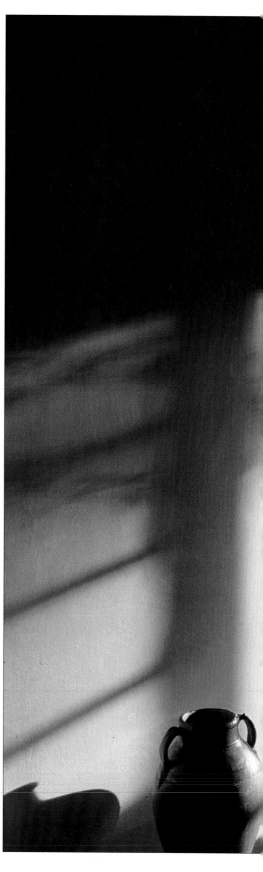

USE SPACE WELL
Left A table and chairs, set in a hallway beside french doors that open onto a garden, makes good use of what might otherwise be just a way to get from one part of the house to another.

INVITE OUTSIDE IN
Right Throw open doors and windows whenever the weather allows, since letting in sunshine and fresh air will boost your feelings of physical and emotional well-being.

Our home is an extension of ourselves, expressing

our interests and beliefs even when we aren't there.

From grand house to townhouse, countryside to city, a home is not simply about setting a scene, following a style, or creating a monument to status and good taste; it is the essential framework around which your life revolves, day in and day out.

In the past, great attention was given to how interiors *looked* and less to how they made us *feel*. As sensuous beings, we need to celebrate the senses through which we both experience and interpret the world; and to constantly exercise our gifts of sight, hearing, touch, taste, and smell lest they become dormant from disuse. Increasingly, as much of living is standardized, the places we inhabit are profoundly *un*sensuous. Work environments have their particular problems: fluorescent light causes headaches and lethargy, air conditioning necessitates sealed windows, unsuitable furniture stresses the body, and there is little care for comfort or room for privacy. By contrast, home is more than ever sweet, since here we can choose the way we want to be, and take steps to redress the balance between the unappealing aspects of our environment and the sensuous experience we seek.

ALL IN ORDER
Above Small rooms work most comfortably when the furniture is to scale and necessities are kept neatly in their place.

SURE HAND
Below A spare interior needs a confident sense of your own style as well as meticulously chosen furnishings and objects.

Nostalgia – if not a solution – is not a straightforward rejection of technology or a denial of progress either; we all appreciate the benefits of electric light, indoor plumbing, central heating, and appliances that save work and time. Rather, we look to the past for the elusive sense of comfort and well-being that is felt missing in the present but cannot be recaptured in period decor or antiques. In the last hundred years, we have significantly changed our eating habits, speech, manners, customs – and we need to go forward rather than back. Nostalgia is rightly absent from most aspects of daily life, yet still we look to the past as a time of greater ease. The comfort of home is enshrined in this view of times past. By taking the best of both present and past, we *can* create the kind of home we want and need – a place that reflects our individual tastes and personalities, where we can retreat from the stress of modern living and be at ease.

We spend our lives trying to make a home – renting, buying, perhaps even building, and moving from one to another as time and fortune dictate. Homemaking is a journey of gradual

PRIVATE PLACE
Above A quiet corner of a bedroom is the perfect place to sit and read or take your ease from the hurly-burly of daily life.

PURPOSE BUILT
Below Suiting form to function, a simple, cozy bed is accommodated in the awkwardly shaped space under the eaves.

experimentation, and we must have common-sense and vision to find and create the place of our dreams. Few things are as enchanting, or as quietly intimate, as the feeling of being at home. So whatever it takes to make that place home is worth it. The daily work that helps give our lives focus is a primary gift of home, since it is always time to repair a lock, clean a rug, freshen the paintwork, or prune a plant. Many of us will gladly paint ceilings, wallpaper rooms, and perform the daily household tasks, but have forgotten how to make a house warm and welcoming. When we truly inhabit a place, we enter into the give and take of homemaking. Choosing paint, polishing a floor, or fixing a fuse satisfy our practical needs as well as contributing to the maintenance of our home. Its charm and comfort may have little to do with expense. Windows draped with quantities of inexpensive cotton muslin speak of wholeheartedness in ways that wisps of costly silk could never match.

Homemaking cannot be forced, but you can approach the decor and furnishing of your house in a generous spirit, and find richness in what you can afford – and in the investment of time and energy. Start by getting the basics right, shaping what *space* you have to meet your needs. Remember that *light* and *air* are necessary for your well-being, and that a house must breathe to be healthy. Use *color* to set the tone of a room and reinforce its purpose: red energizes a library for lively intellectual exchange, sky-blue soothes in a bedroom. Choose natural and sustainable materials, such as bamboo and jute, and appreciate their *surface* texture and variation of color. Acknowledge that silence is

COLOR INSPIRATION
Above & left Something as simple as a bowl of olives might have been the starting point for the successful combining of colors in this kitchen.

APPRECIATE THE OLD
Top right Practical as well as beautiful, this dressing room is home to a 1930s' shop display unit and capacious closets made from recycled oak.

THEME & VARIATION
Right Here, bold colors and textures are echoed in the Lloyd loom chair, floor coverings, and wall treatment to create a scheme with integrity.

sometimes golden, and buy appliances that have the quietest *sound*. Avoid embellishment at first in favor of function: if you need a bed, get a good mattress rather than fancy sheets. Recall the natural world and celebrate your senses in a home enriched with the scents, textures, sounds, and colors that appeal to you.

In a world of rapid, often uncomfortable, change, we need more than ever to feel the security and comfort of home. That's part of the reason the Creative Home Arts Club exists! So set aside fashion, apply your faculties, put the talent of your mind and the skill of your hands to work, and embrace *New Decorator* to create a home that combines well-being and style and meets your needs.

NEW TRADITIONS
Above Settlers in the New World painted barns in a color now called "barn red," as on these kitchen cabinets. You can have your own version of this color, or any other, by making *Homegrown milk paint* (see pages 88–89).

BROADEN YOUR MIND
Right The vine-covered terrace of a Tuscan villa is just right for enjoying a convivial lunch outdoors. Take every opportunity that is presented to you to travel and absorb new experiences, since they will enrich your own life and that of your home.

Space

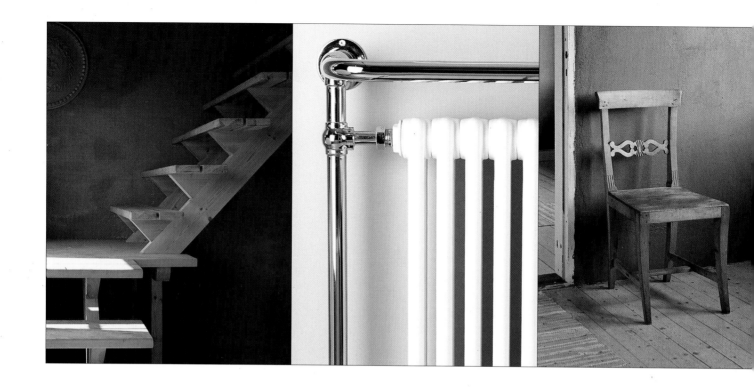

Thinking about space

REGARDLESS OF DIMENSIONS and aesthetics, a home should be a refuge; serene, comfortable, and safe in an ever-changing world. Most people are very happy with their homes, but it is worth the time and effort to reconsider the space you have, now and again, so that it reflects and meets your changing needs.

Start by thinking about your home in its entirety to appreciate how rooms relate to each other, and to the world outside; after all, neither rooms nor house exist in isolation. Let rooms echo the orderliness of nature by careful planning and organization. Before

changing any room, ask yourself how it makes you feel. Are you comfortable or uneasy? What aspects are pleasing? What have you learned to tolerate and live with? What do you really dislike? It may even be useful to empty an unsatisfactory room completely, and then reassess it without distracting detail.

Space is an expensive, precious thing, especially in the city, and few people can afford as much of it as they would like. Make the most of the space you call home, even if it is tiny, rented, or borrowed, in the knowledge that virtually nothing is impossible in

Time and space – time to be alone, space to move

a place that is yours to mold to your needs. Walls should provide both physical and emotional shelter rather than making you feel confined.

The quality and perception of space can always be manipulated until they bear little relationship to the real dimensions of a room. Free-standing folding screens and sliding doors are invaluable devices for dividing space, defining areas of different activity in an open-plan space or bringing intimate corners to a room. Decorative tricks, such as stripes or pattern, fool the eye to make space seem larger or smaller.

Be alive to what is appropriate for you, independent of style and fashion. If you love minimalism, go for it, but be aware that you will probably need a lot of additional storage space unless you can cut down on clutter. Most people accumulate objects and treasures, filling their home with possessions that reflect their energy, imagination, and enthusiasms. Even if you are an inveterate hoarder, a disciplined approach to accessibility and long-term storage will help to keep your home efficient and in order. Your space is what you make it: remember this and shape it as you will.

about – may become the scarcities of tomorrow.

Edwin Way Teale

Large space

DEFINED BY COLOR
Where internal dividing walls have been removed, areas of different activity are clearly defined by the bold use of strong color in cabinets and furniture.

THE DECORATIVE SCOPE and design flexibility that large space allows is counterbalanced by a greater margin for error. Careful planning is needed to avoid dead space, and it is important to choose unifying materials and design details so that living areas do not appear uncomfortably fragmented or empty.

Balance privacy with openness by providing places for comfortable retreat alongside communal areas for meeting, talking, and entertaining. Having space is a luxury, but everybody needs their own corner where they can relax in solitude and peace. In large rooms with many functions, it is reassuring to have distinct areas for different activities. Consider the particular value of focal points as well. A dramatic painting or sculptural plant will hold the attention and help to define the character of your space.

CREATING UNITY
Right The twin levels of this lofty space are pulled together by vast windows divided by glazing bars. Boarded walls, handrails, and exposed floor joists repeat the linear theme.

PUNCTUATION POINTS
Below left Framed textiles and huge cacti punctuate the fluid space of a long gallery. Neutral tones in the background heighten the arresting effect.

REDUCING ECHO
Below right Oak beams and furniture of solid wood act as baffles to absorb resonance in an open-plan kitchen with high-pitched ceiling.

The most effective spaces are often not designed

but have evolved over time in response to need.

Small space

INGENUITY, FLEXIBILITY, AND lateral thinking are your best allies when planning a small space. Consider its restrictions from a positive point of view (less chance to make an error; less expensive to put one right), and be assured that your needs are more important than design conventions and decorating trends.

For inspiration, look to the compact interior of a ship's cabin, or the sleeping compartment of a train. Here, living is at the closest of quarters, but the very utility of these finely detailed spaces has a unique and enduring appeal. Physical boundaries need not limit the comfort of small rooms if you plan and organize them with care. To encourage their natural intimacy and avoid any feeling of enclosure, keep continuity in color and detail, and ensure ease of movement.

CLASSIC DESIGN
Above These curvaceous wooden stools stack for convenient, space-saving storage. Their pleasing design is a classic, happy combination of simple style and practicality.

STRAIGHT LINES
The uncompromising lines of the room are followed through in the furnishings.

GRAND ILLUSIONS
Use narrow floorboards to open out a limited area.

Expand what

LITERARY PLATFORM
Elevated above the floor, an orderly library is furnished with a comfortable chair.

CONCEALED STORAGE
Open stairs give access to a platform that has concealed storage space at floor level.

PALE BUT INTERESTING
Left This neat apartment gets its feeling of calm cohesion with the use of light wood, creamy soft furnishings, and white paintwork. The footstool and sofa throws add bold color accents to prevent too bland an appearance.

UNOBSTRUCTED VIEW
Left No fussy furnishings
or objects impede either
view or movement in this
multifunctional space.
Areas for cooking, eating,
and relaxing are brought
together and defined by
complementary colors,
textures, and finishes that
reinforce the uncluttered
character of the room.

KEEP IT SIMPLE
- Think in terms of
  continuity, and unify
  decorative details.
- Forget exuberant
  or layered patterns.
- Choose versatile
  furniture that suits
  more than one room
  and is easy to move.

space you have by thinking positively about it.

OPEN DISPLAY
Left Careful organization
is vital if small space is to
function well. In this tiny
kitchen, frequently used
dishes are close at hand
on open shelving while
folding chairs are hung
neatly out of the way on
the side of a cupboard.

BREAKING THE RULES
Right A change of scale
works surprisingly well in
a small bathroom where
the furnishings dominate
the room. Strong shapes,
clean lines, and a degree
of confidence are needed
to pull off the marriage
of large with small.

Shaping space

SLIDING GLASS PANELS
A sliding wall of opaque glass defines and screens a bathing area, creating private space that is not cut off from the rest of the apartment.

A HOUSE THAT FUNCTIONS well is easily maintained, efficient to run, and comfortable to live in. Shaping a space to fulfill this ideal means understanding how you want to live rather than sticking to conventional ideas of how a home should be. Take stock of your home to help you to clarify what you like and dislike about it, and what you would like to change.

Whatever the size of their home, most people feel that they do not have enough space. Relocating is an option, but a disruptive and expensive one. It makes sense, therefore, to look for ways to improve on what you have and increase your feeling of space, even if physical boundaries seem limiting. Assess each room in turn. Your main considerations should be its size, use, and how many hours you spend in it each day.

How *you* want

CREATING A WORKING PLAN
Sketching a floor plan of a room, or taking a Polaroid photograph of it, can be a great help in seeing it from a fresh perspective. Use the annotations on the drawing below to make a checklist, then refer to it when you come to assess how well a room functions.

NATURAL LIGHT
Plentiful daylight will enhance any space. Keep windows clear if possible.

FINE DIVISION
Right Richly decorated on one side, restrained on the other, an ebony screen is the dramatic divide between living and sleeping spaces in this elegant interior.

CONTRASTING ELEMENTS
Pale colors are light relief against the dark screen.

FEATURES
Fixed features add character and are best retained.

SPACE DIVIDERS
In multifunctional rooms, it is essential to balance privacy with openness.

STOP & THINK
• If at all practical, consider making the largest room the one in which you spend the most time.

• Walk through the rooms in your mind, assessing how you use them at different times and seasons.

• Think of storage needs as an integral part of a room plan.

IN & OUT
Easy movement and a free flow of traffic are as important as space.

IRREGULAR PROPORTIONS
Awkward angles can become a positive feature when used to define areas of activity.

to live is more important than style conventions.

CURVED HALF WALL
Above left In open-plan space, it is important to define areas of activity. This low wall cradles a dining table and chairs, and its sweeping lines echo the ceiling recess.

LOFTY VISTAS
Above center A soaring glazed doorway, open stairs, and colors in complementary tones help to accentuate the lofty grandeur of these connecting rooms.

DINING ISLAND
Above right A sparsely furnished kitchen and dining room vibrates with bold color that breaks up the space, making its proportions seem generous rather than overwhelming.

TEXTURAL INTEREST
Where colors need to be kept neutral, textures can play an important role in adding variety and interest.

Double-sided screen

MATCH patterned and plain fabrics to give the screen two different personalities.

AN OLD WOODEN SCREEN is easy to re-cover, or you could buy one of the widely available ready-made screens and substitute your own fabric. When choosing fabric, consider how you will use the screen. Delicate light-diffusing partitions of voile or embroidered net would be perfect to shade a window, while a more robust fabric, such as canvas, would be suitable to screen a secluded workspace, conceal clutter for instant if illusory order, or create a private corner. To make a room more flexible, and movement through it more fluid, use several screens together to divide and change the space at will.

1 Place the screen on a firm work surface. For an old screen, unscrew the hinges (replace if rusted), and remove all traces of old fabric, paper, and nails. Wipe the panels clean. For a new screen, simply remove the fabric. To make reassembly easier, number the panels in order on both sides.

2 Cut the decorative fabric slightly larger than the panel. Stretch the fabric over the frame, and secure by tacking with gimp pins at intervals (or use a staple gun). Ensure that the weave is straight, and consider the pattern repeat across the panels.

3 Now cover the other side of the panel. Cut the plain fabric to the size of the panel, allowing an extra 2in (5cm) to turn under. Turn the extra fabric under to hide the raw edges and secure by tacking with gimp pins (or staples).

4 Cut a wide strip of contrasting fabric to edge the panel and cover the panel sides. Place the fabric slightly in from one long side edge, then lay upholsterer's tape along the outside edge of the fabric. Tack down with gimp pins (or staples).

5 Fold the fabric up over the tape to cover the panel edge and secure it with tacks. Fold the raw edges under along the panel side and secure with gimp pins. Finish the other long edge and side, then the top. Finish the base last, ensuring that the fabric fits neatly under it for stability.

6 Use decorative tacks to cover the gimp pins along the panel edges; the panel is now complete. Set it aside while you cover and finish the other panels in the same way. Finally, reassemble the screen by hinging the three panels together in order according to your numbering.

Painting stripes

WHETHER BROAD OR NARROW, crisply delineated or softly edged, stripes are always of the moment. Free association places them conveniently in both formal and relaxed settings, recalling the upright dignity of the pin-striped suit, the cheery casualness of awning and deck-chair canvas. Stripes exist in most cultures, and are a natural and attractive element of exposed wooden floorboards, tongue-and-groove paneling, wainscoting, chair, and dado rails. Stripes can create a variety of optical illusions. Long, narrow ones give height to a low-ceilinged room; broad horizontal ones hug it in an intimate embrace. Try painting your own stripes by hand, roughly, if you like, for naive charm.

PREPARING THE SURFACE
Stripes highlight any irregularities in the surface, so make sure it is smooth if you want them to be sharp at the edges. Apply a base coat of paint, and leave to dry.

◄ STEP 1: APPLY MASKING TAPE
Apply strips of tape to the wall, spaced close together for narrow stripes, far apart for wide ones.

STEP 2: PAINT OVER THE TAPE ►
Rub down the sides of each strip of masking tape to make sure it is firmly adhering to the surface. Paint right over the masking tape, using long vertical brush strokes so that the paint is not forced under the edges of the tape. Leave to dry. Stripes painted onto a dark base may need a second coat.

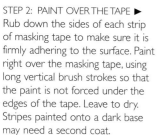

◄ STEP 3: PEEL OFF THE TAPE
When the paint is thoroughly dry, carefully peel off all the strips of masking tape. Start at the top and work down to the bottom, using a steady movement, to reveal the clearly defined stripes beneath.

Free-hanging wooden shelf

CLOTHESLINE and nautical ropes are good for hanging the heavy wooden shelf.

ANYONE CAN MAKE this hanging shelf, since only the most basic carpentry skills and tools are needed. Choose reclaimed wooden floorboards or roughly hewn planks for their rustic appeal, or use highly polished machine-finished timber as a sophisticated alternative. The shelf may be hung by lengths of rope (as here) or brightly colored thick cord from beams, or by wire with metal eyelets from hooks screwed into ceiling joists. Placed above a table or work surface, the shelf provides extra space for everyday utensils to be stored within reach, but it is equally at home as a pleasing place to display potted plants.

WHAT YOU NEED

PIECE OF TIMBER

CHINAGRAPH PENCIL
(FROM ART SHOPS)

ELECTRIC DRILL &
FLAT BIT ATTACHMENT

TENON SAW

SANDPAPER
(COARSE & FINE)

ROPE

ADHESIVE TAPE

COARSE STRING

1 Select a piece of timber for the shelf and the rope by which to hang it. Consider where you will hang the shelf and how you will use it. The rope must be sturdy enough to support both the weight of the timber and the contents of the shelf.

3 Use a tenon saw to cut from the edge of the timber to one of the drilled holes, then around the hole to form a notch with three squared sides. Each notch should be a bit wider than the diameter of the rope; try out the rope to test it. Form the other notches in the same way.

5 Cut one piece of rope for each support (the length depends on the shelf height) and fold to form a loop. Join the rope with two pieces of tape 6in (15cm) apart. Bind string around and form a loop, as shown. Holding the free end with one hand, bind string tightly over the loop to secure it.

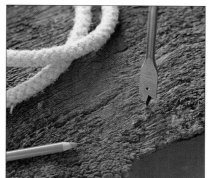

2 To hang the shelf, the rope is held in notches cut on the two long sides of the timber. A piece of timber 39in (1m) long needs two holes on each side. Mark drill holes to start the notches directly opposite each other, then drill out the holes.

4 Roll a small piece of coarse sandpaper into a cylinder shape and rub back and forth against the rough inside edges of the notches to smooth them. Repeat with fresh pieces of sandpaper as needed, then finish off with rolls of fine sandpaper until the edges are completely smooth.

6 When you reach the end of the loop, cut the string, leaving a long end. Thread through the loop, then pull up sharply on the opposite free end to secure the long end within the bound portion. Place the shelf between the lower loops, and slot the rope into the notches.

Minimalism

LONG BEFORE THE word minimalism was coined for the style of that name, William Morris (champion of the Arts and Crafts movement) urged: *Have nothing in your houses that you do not know to be useful or believe to be beautiful* – a wise counsel that is as appropriate today as it was in the nineteenth century.

At its most extreme, minimalism is a hard row to hoe, but defining it as *imparting an impression of space through unfussy design and decorative detail* makes it seem more achievable. Having room to breathe in your home is conducive to health, serenity, and well-being, and the absence of what is neither useful nor seen to be beautiful is a sure way to create a tranquil refuge. If you want to try this style, you can apply it simply in the form of furniture with clean lines and objects specifically chosen for their contribution to a room.

PURE PERFECTION
Right Natural materials, including slate, cast iron, brick, stone, leather, and chrome are unadorned, and shine gloriously in this great room, which is further enhanced by the play of light and shadow.

LETTING LIGHT IN
Floor-to-ceiling glazed double doors maximize all the available light.

GOOD CONNECTION
The outer brickwork is echoed in the arching inner walls, so forming a continuity between outside and in.

HARD WITH SOFT
Below Uncluttered, light, and pared to the essence of what a kitchen needs, this inviting model bears the mark of minimalism. A picture, done in chalky pastels, softens the view.

Monochrome schemes and restrained decoration induce easeful harmony.

EYE FOR DETAIL
Far left Wainscoting, woodwork, bath: here all is white, except for the considered detail of tiny black squares, set in serried ranks on the white flooring.

KEEPING FAITH
Left Minimalism can be applied equally to rustic interiors, and still retain a sensuous simplicity. In this harmonious cottage bedroom, the senses are at once gratified by the sweep of tented net and the seagreen woodwork.

STYLE POINTERS

• Use your largest rooms for living and entertaining, smaller ones for privacy. A sense of space is the essence of the style.

• Think in terms of unbroken lines from floor to ceiling.

• Wrap floors, walls, and ceilings in one color, or use subtle translucent shades of a single color.

• Let light flood in; do without window coverings if you can.

Ordered clutter

IN THEIR PLACE
Stacked on shelves and hung from hooks above the worktop, these pots, pans, and other cooking utensils form an orderly, practical display within easy reach of the cook.

THERE ARE NO two ways about it – you either loathe or love clutter. For these opposing camps, having *stuff* around is as uncomfortable for the one as its absence is for the other. But it makes sense to be surrounded by the things that mean most to you, particularly if you view home as an extension of yourself.

Treasured possessions are every bit as important as the room (or rooms) in which they are arrayed. They can complete a decorative scheme, or transform an unexceptional part of the house into a special place. You can personalize a space (vital for those living in rented accommodation) and lift your spirits all in one go by displaying favored belongings to express your enthusiasms and passions. In this way, you will feel at home – and because you do, others will too.

THEME & VARIATION
Carry the color theme of a room right through to its decorative accessories.

BACK TO BASICS
Left Neatly folded items, piled and ranged along shelves, are a testament to the most basic law of clutter: keep it in check. The hand-woven baskets and mementos add the necessary personal note.

ELEMENTARY SUMS
Right Patterns, textures, furnishings, colors, and objects all enhance each other in this living room. The elements combine to stimulate and delight, giving the room a sense of comfortable cohesion.

Keep the accessories of

DIVIDE & CONQUER
Above With open storage, group items of the same kind together to prevent disorder. Here, a dresser beside an exterior door has small compartments at floor level for garden footwear and gear.

REST FOR THE EYE
An impressive fireplace and mantel are a tranquil focus amid the room's busyness.

VISUAL ABUNDANCE
Side chairs are upholstered in complementary fabrics: a plump cushion and woolen throw add yet more layers.

VITAL PRINCIPLES

• Clutter run riot is nothing more than a jumble. Never let it get out of hand; it will overwhelm you.

• Choose matching or complementary colors to avoid a disjointed effect. Keep backgrounds plain or neutral.

• Discipline display storage by grouping items together.

daily life within view, to be appreciated and used.

Kitchen cupboard restoration

SEARCH garages and attics for an old cupboard that still has some life left in it.

DON'T GIVE UP ON an elderly cupboard that has staunchly stood the test of time, despite much wear and tear. Instead, consider restoring it. Apply new paint in a toning color on top of the old; then, to emphasize the charm of age, distress the piece by gently sanding away the new paint so that the original color, partly revealed, blends with the new. Coarsely grained wood, such as pine, with well-defined knots, is best for this technique. Finally, paint the inside of the cupboard in a contrasting color and line the shelf with a vibrant vinyl shelf liner for a finish that is both colorful and serviceable.

1 Remove the door knob and set aside (clean and polish it if necessary). Use a heavy craft knife to cut away the old wire mesh. Brush out any debris, then wash the cupboard inside and out with warm, soapy water. Leave the cupboard to dry at least overnight before continuing.

2 For a more interesting effect when the piece is distressed, choose an emulsion paint in a color that contrasts with the original paint. Apply one coat to the outside of the cupboard and allow to dry. Apply a second coat and allow to dry overnight.

3 Use coarse sandpaper on the outside of the cupboard to rub down the new paint so that the old paint is revealed in places (wrapping the sandpaper around a wood block may help). Take care to follow the grain of the wood, and avoid rubbing too hard. Finish with fine sandpaper.

4 Make sure the inside of the cupboard is thoroughly clean and dry. Sand lightly and brush out any debris. Apply the undercoat; allow to dry. Apply one coat of emulsion and allow to dry. Cut the vinyl shelf liner to fit, and add decorative tacks along the front edge, if desired.

5 Replace the door knob. Cut a piece of wire mesh, using wire cutters, slightly larger than the door, and attach it to the front of the door with staples (or a staple gun). Cover the raw edges of the wire mesh with narrow battens, glued and nailed to fix them in place.

6 The cupboard is now complete. To protect its paint finish and nourish any exposed wood, apply rosemary beeswax polish (see pages 140–141) to the outside. Use a clean, lint-free, soft cloth to rub the polish in, then buff to a gentle sheen with a fresh, clean, lint-free, soft cloth.

Accessibility & storage

IT IS EASY TO ANTICIPATE storage requirements in a room with a dedicated function, such as a bathroom. Where the room is the center of different activities, however, it is worth considering varied and changing individual needs so that what is used often on hand, and what is seldom used is stored out of the way.

A kitchen is just such a room. Here, people cook, eat, wash dishes, relax, read, do homework, laundry, or simply gather to pass the time of day. Organizing storage close to its associated activity saves time and energy, and stops annoyances from accumulating into stress. So, put the once-a-year dinner service in high-level china cabinets, store pots and pans in low-level cupboards beside the stove, and throw out the goofy gadgets gathering dust at the backs of drawers.

GLAZED CUPBOARD
Bowls, plates, saucers, and other everyday crockery is stacked in a wall-hung glazed cupboard close to the dining table, where it is instantly accessible for family meals.

CHILDREN'S PLAY AREA – A LIBRARY FOR THE COOKS
At the other end of the family kitchen shown at right, books for the children fill a stone alcove and a toy farm is set up, always ready for play. Through the open door, an easy chair in the hallway library is the perfect place to relax while selecting a recipe for dinner.

LONG-TERM STORAGE
Wooden window seats hold bundles of neatly folded and beribboned table linen. The hinged seats, hidden beneath well-padded cushions, store pieces of infrequently used kitchen equipment as well.

A FAMILY KITCHEN: COMFORT WITH PRACTICALITY

Every corner of this small family kitchen has been used to meet the practical needs of its occupants, making it a welcoming refuge besides an efficient workplace. Open shelves, cupboards, and storage bins under the window seat give easy access to everything a convivial family needs for cooking, eating, and enjoying life together.

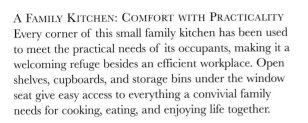

OPEN SHELF DISPLAY
Short and tall ceramic jugs can be accommodated on shelves that are staggered in height and of varying lengths. The highly decorative jugs make an eye-catching display when they are not in use.

TABLE-END DRAWERS
The underside of the table is put to good use with two narrow drawers fitted neatly into its frame. The drawer at one end contains napkins: each member of the family has their own, rolled into its own ring. Everyday cutlery is housed at the other end.

HIDDEN UTILITY AREA
Beneath the sink, a versatile storage area hides behind a pair of curtains, hung from a chrome pole. There is room for brushes, pails, and other cleaning materials alongside the big aluminum trash can.

Collectibles shadow box

REMEMBER nature's glory in a display of decorative seedheads and pods.

IF YOUR DRAWERS are packed with treasures and every surface is overflowing with precious clutter, this project is custom-made for you. A shadow box (a sealed wooden box with a protective glass cover) is the perfect place to house a prized collection or delicate mementos. It is not as difficult to make as you might think: most local hardware stores will be happy to cut wood according to your specifications, and to cut glass and hardboard to size for you as well. Repositionable mountboard (available from picture framers) allows you to display chosen objects against any background you wish, including fabric or handmade papers.

WHAT YOU NEED

REPOSITIONABLE MOUNTBOARD

DISPLAY BACKGROUND

MULTIPURPOSE GLUE

WOOD FOR FRAME & BEADING

MASKING & PAPER TAPE

DANISH OIL

BEESWAX POLISH

GLASS & HARDBOARD

BRADAWL & SCREWS

1 Have the mountboard and background cut to size. Peel the surface away from the mountboard, and then carefully position the background on top of this tacky surface. Rub down so that the background sticks firmly. Arrange the chosen objects on the board, glue in place, and allow to dry.

3 The front of the box is neatly finished with beading, which should be mitred at the ends. Use multipurpose glue to fix the beading to the frame, then secure with masking tape, and allow to dry in a warm, airy place overnight. Remove all the masking tape from the frame.

5 Keeping the frame still face down, place the mountboard face down in the recess provided; lay the hardboard back plate over it. Use a pencil to mark evenly spaced holes for the fixing screws, then start off the holes with a bradawl. Screw the boards firmly in position to the frame.

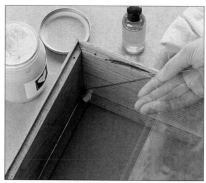

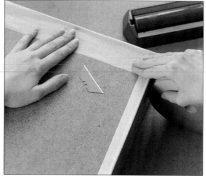

2 Buy wood for the four sides of the box and have a recess cut along each piece to hold the mountboard and back plate. Have the ends mitred so that the corners fit snugly. Use multipurpose glue to assemble the frame, then secure with masking tape until dry.

4 Use a clean soft cloth to apply a light coat of Danish oil to the outside of the frame, then follow with one application of beeswax polish (see page 140). Lay the frame face down and dab a little glue in each of the inner corners. Lower the glass into the frame, and press down lightly.

6 Seal the back of the frame with masking tape to prevent dust from entering, then finish the edges with brown paper tape (if necessary, use a heavy craft knife to trim the edges). Turn the frame over and polish the glass with a clean soft cloth to remove any finger marks.

Light

Thinking about light

WITHOUT LIGHT THERE would be no life: plants and people alike flourish according to how much or how little daylight they receive. We should all watch the sun rise or set occasionally, and although we can no longer live by the rhythms of the sun and moon, we can orient rooms to take advantage of daylight, and so make our homes more natural and healthy.

To appreciate how light and dark, shadow and shade can modify space and affect atmosphere and mood, try forgoing electric light for a day. Observe how the constant variations of light tone, intensity, and color transform your surroundings. Note the gray-on-gray of shadows, and the interplay of light and shade. At dusk, light candles and table lamps to observe how artificial light changes the effect.

Natural light stimulates the brain and hormones so that your unconscious instinct is to be awake and alert during daylight hours, to rest and sleep when it is dark. In northern latitudes during the dark season, the suicide rate soars. Some people are so affected by low-light conditions that they suffer from what is now termed *seasonal affective disorder*, characterized by

Let the form of an object be what it may: light,

depression and fatigue. Daily doses of full-spectrum lighting – which mimics natural light – can help to correct the condition. Light therapy is being used to treat psoriasis (a chronic but not life-threatening skin complaint), schizophrenia, and some cancers as well. Try to spend some time outside each day, even if it is overcast or cloudy. Your energy levels will rise, and you will feel happier for it.

Shadow and shade are also essential for comfort, health, and well-being, but many homes lack vitality simply because of low light levels. After dark and on dull days, you will need artificial light so that rooms can be fully used. A good lighting plan combines soft background illumination with task lighting directed at the work on hand – preparing a meal, reading a book, or whatever. Accent lighting throws decorative details and objects of interest into relief, bringing personality and character to a room. Light thus has an important role to play in creating a home that feels right, and is comfortable. Balance considerations of mood, taste, and practicality to enjoy your home in the very best light. It will make all the difference.

shade, perspective will always make it beautiful.

John Constable

Atmosphere & mood

IN THE GLOAMING
Within the safe enclosure of pierced iron lanterns, lit candles are a pleasant way to brighten the dusk.

THIS LIVING ROOM, pictured first on a sunny morning and then at night, illustrates how natural and artificial light can be advantageously used to suggest different moods for day and evening. Sunlight spills in through open doors and windows from its first morning rays until twilight, and the room is alive with its energy. At night, with the curtains closed and a wood fire ablaze, pools of yellow lamplight suggest quiet activities, such as reading a book, while shadowy corners encourage thoughtful conversation and peaceful repose.

DAYLIGHT VITALITY
Right & below It is vital to maximize sunlight and natural light, particularly at times when both are scarce. The availability of natural light can even determine the use of a room: thinking is clearer and eyes are more rested in natural light. Support it with efficient artificial light, if necessary, and use blinds or shutters to reduce stressful glare.

BENEFICIAL CONTRAST
Shadow is a necessary and restful contrast to sunlight.

LIGHT & FRESH AIR
Open interior doors to let in fresh air as well as light.

REFLECTED LIGHT
A white ceiling relects light, whatever a room's decor.

CLEAR VISION
Keep windows sparkling clean to maximize daylight.

EVENING RETREAT
Left & below The change from day to evening is marked by firelight and glowing lamps. Dancing patterns and variations of light and shadow fill the room with a peaceful atmosphere, and enliven its decor. Warm colors, such as the magenta red and golden yellow used here, enhance the sense of comfort and coziness in this evening retreat.

LIGHT & DARK
• During daylight hours, pull coverings clear of windows.

• Use half curtains (also known as café curtains) where you need privacy, and to diffuse light and stop or reduce glare.

• Consider blackout lining for curtains if you need to shut out light in a room.

SHADOWY LIGHT
Lamplight and firelight cast soft shadows of repose.

CHEERFUL COLOR
A bright patchwork door curtain adds a cheery note.

TIME FOR LEISURE
Dim corners invite intimacy and encourage relaxation.

SAFE & SOUND
Draw heavy lined curtains as a shield against the night.

Illuminating a room

THE AIM OF GOOD lighting is to blend light, shadow, and shade, balancing considerations of practicality and comfort with atmosphere and mood to create a stimulating environment of varied textures; getting it right can be almost a revelation.

Choose lighting that is flexible and can easily be adapted to accommodate changing preferences and needs – to be welcoming, inviting, and relaxing, as well as appropriate for all your activities, whether at work or rest. For artificial light (see pages 56–57), a combination of background, accent, and task lighting fulfills most requirements, but there is no satisfactory substitute for the pure energy that daylight and sunlight deliver. Finally, remember the light of candles and firelight: it is always cheering.

DECORATIVE LIGHTING
Evocative sources of gently filtered low-level light leave warm pools on the floor and brighten dark corners. The delicate lamp shades, made from goatskin with patterns of henna, contrast with the striking solidity of the carved furniture.

VIEW THROUGH TO KITCHEN, WITH MIRROR
A vast mirror, outlined with rough-hewn planks and suspended on sturdy chains, frames garden greenery beyond the facing windows, and reflects and draws light from outside into the room. Its surface multiplies the light and is flatteringly tinted to enhance the mood.

FIRELIGHT
Leaping flames and glowing embers encourage a feeling of hospitable intimacy in the room as well as lightening the mood with their warmth and brightness.

LIGHT TOUCH IN A PARTY ROOM
Opening onto a secluded garden, this room is ideal for entertaining. Generous window space provides a firm visual link with outdoors, and the sheen of polished plaster walls and ceiling bounces as much light as possible back into the room.

REFLECTIVE SURFACES
Copper shows through in patches on a worn silver-plate tray, and adds its own reflection to an appealing collection of clear glass and anemones with translucent petals. Tiny spotlights set into the iridescent ceiling bring the whole to life.

NATURAL LIGHT
Fabric blinds can be pulled down to softly diffuse strong sunlight so that it comes into the room at a gentle angle. For maximum light, they are rolled up all the way.

PIERCED LANTERNS
Glowing candle lamps are clustered on a dark polished wood table, which is placed close to a comfortable sofa. Their flickering patterns of golden light make a striking focal point in the room.

PALE FURNISHINGS
Unbleached natural canvas and cream cushions, placed against polished plaster walls, help to illuminate that part of the room that benefits least from natural light.

Rolled beeswax candles

ROLLING MALLEABLE sheets of wax around a wick is a quick and easy way to make candles. Beeswax is sweetly fragrant, and the wax sheets are attractively patterned with raised hexagons, but you could use paraffin wax if you prefer. This is a good project for children to do with adult supervision, and you can omit the fourth step, although the candles will burn better if the wick is coated with wax. Tall candles make a grand display in elegant branched holders of silver or crystal: add luster or glass droplets, known as *bobèches*, for even more sparkle. Shorter candles look charming set in unpretentious holders of pottery, iron, or glass.

THE TRADITIONAL honey color of beeswax brings a comforting glow to a room.

WHAT YOU NEED

BEESWAX CHUNK

CHOPPING BOARD

SHARP KITCHEN KNIFE

HEATPROOF CONTAINER

SCISSORS OR CRAFT KNIFE

BEESWAX OR PARAFFIN WAX SHEETS

½IN (12MM) WICK

1 Set the beeswax chunk on a chopping board and slice off several small pieces with a sharp kitchen knife. Put the pieces into a heatproof container, then set it aside for Step 4. Use scissors or a craft knife to cut a sheet of wax into a rectangle: the shorter sides should be the height you want the candle to be. Cut the wick ¾in (20mm) longer than the short sides of the wax sheet.

2 Lay the wick on the wax sheet along one of its short sides, aligning the end of the wick with the bottom of the sheet. Gently press the wick into the wax, and then roll the wax as tightly as possible around the wick. Continue rolling until you reach the end of the sheet.

3 If you prefer a thicker candle, add another layer. The second sheet of wax should be the same size as the first. Roll it tightly around the candle as before. If necessary, add more layers until you have the desired thickness. At the end of the final sheet, press down firmly along the edge to secure.

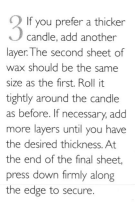

4 If necessary, use a knife to trim the base of the candle so that it is level. To coat the wick with wax, set the small pieces of wax from Step 1 in their heatproof container over a gentle flame or over a pan of simmering water until melted. Remove from the heat, dip the wick into the melted wax, and then roll it around until thoroughly coated. Stand the candle upright in a cool place so that the wax can harden.

Natural light

PRIVACY WITH LIGHT
The lower panes of this bathroom window are made from sandblasted glass, which filters harsh light and allows privacy. The whole window has been left clear to let in maximum daylight.

HUMAN BEINGS FLOURISH in direct relation to their exposure to light. Natural light and sunlight lift the spirits and give a brilliance to life that enhances all its aspects. Light deprivation is today even recognized as a medical condition, so aptly named SAD – seasonal affective disorder, or "winter blues."

When thinking about natural light in your home, remember that north-facing rooms receive little or no sun and south-facing ones get most. Observe where sun comes in at different times of day, heeding the natural cycle of dark and light: it makes no sense to be in a gloomy room if another has good light. You can never have too many windows, even if keeping them clean is a chore. Skylights can be beneficial in dark upper levels. Before having one installed, check to see if planning permission is required.

While natural light is vital for life, shade and shadows bring repose.

KEEPING CONTROL
Roller blinds covering an expanse of glass provide an easy means of controlling light during the day.

WINTER BLUES

• Seasonal affective disorder (SAD) is a depressive state that results from severe lack of natural light.

• Every day, try to spend some time in natural light outside.

• Try taking extract of St. John's Wort. If you take it regularly, it can help to relieve mild depression.

MORNING CALL
Left The day begins in a positive, dynamic mood when morning light can spill into the bedroom. Protect fabrics from the fading and weakening effects of bright sunlight by fitting opaque blinds.

GENTLE DRAMA
Right Small space seems larger when filled with sunlight, throwing detail into relief and drawing the eye to focal points. Here, louvered shutters bring their own dramatic patterns to the timbered walls and fireplace.

SOUTHERN EXPOSURE

Left A wall of windows is wrapped around this indoor veranda. Here is the place to follow the passage of light through the day, and to take full advantage of sunlight at times when it is scarce.

NATURAL ENERGY
Varying intensities of bright sunlight and dappled shade energize your surroundings.

HEALTHY HOME

Below In this kitchen, glazed cupboards reflect and intensify daylight as it streams through open casement windows. Use every means of letting available daylight into your rooms to make the house a more natural and healthy place.

Eyelet pantry curtain

THE FABRIC of the curtain echoes the colors of this charming kitchen utensil jar.

AN OLD PANTRY WINDOW drape was the inspiration for the eyelet heading of this curtain, which you could use to dress any small window, depending on your choice of fabric. For a kitchen or pantry curtain, choose a washable fabric that has some body to it, for example, cotton ticking or crisp canvas. In a bathroom, diaphanous voile would look pretty and also screen an ugly view while letting in light. Loosely gathered and without unnecessary detail, the curtain is a snap to assemble and sew, by hand if you wish. Hang it from a metal or wooden pole by neatly knotted loops of cord or fabric, or by brass curtain rings, as used here.

WHAT YOU NEED

FABRIC
TAPE MEASURE
DRESSMAKER'S PINS
NEEDLE & THREAD
FABRIC PUNCH & DIE
CUTTING BOARD
LARGE BRASS EYELETS
HAMMER
LARGE BRASS
CURTAIN RINGS

1 Put everything needed to make the curtain on a firm surface. The width of the fabric should be one-and-a-half times the length of the curtain pole so that the curtain has fullness. The length depends on the size of the window where the curtain will hang. Allow a little extra for turnings.

2 Turn a narrow double hem along the two side edges of the fabric. Pin and press, then stitch. For the heading, make a hem 4in (10cm) deep at the top edge. Working on a cutting board (or any protective surface), punch evenly spaced holes along the heading.

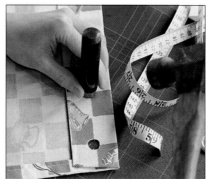

3 The eyelets should be a bit larger in diameter than the holes punched in the heading. To assemble them, hold the male part of one eyelet at the back of the first hole and the female piece at the front. Bring the two parts of the eyelet together with the fabric in between.

4 Hold the two eyelet parts together while you lay the curtain flat on the cutting board. Position the die over the eyelet and, keeping your fingers clear, strike the dye firmly with a hammer so that the eyelet parts lock together. Repeat for the remaining holes and eyelets.

5 To calculate the length of the curtain, hold it up to the curtain pole; put a pin in position to mark the required length. Turn a double hem at the bottom of the curtain, press with an iron, and pin in position. Use a needle and matching thread to neatly slip-stitch the hem. Remove the pins.

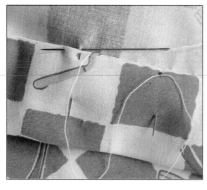

6 Thread a curtain ring through each eyelet. If necessary, bend the rings slightly open so that both rings and curtain can run freely along the curtain pole. Put the pole through the rings and suspend the pole above the window from brackets in the wall.

Hanging a curtain

LEGEND HAS IT that the first curtain was a cloak hung from a sword by a medieval traveler on a cold night. Legend has wit, but we owe the curtains of today to the heavy hangings of four-poster beds that gave the occupants privacy and kept out drafts.

These twin criteria are still good reasons to put curtains on your windows (or even your four-poster) and enhance the comfort of your home. The double drapes here do several things: they frame and dress a window with swaths of fabric that insulate against the cold and strong sun; they obscure an uninspiring view; and their elegance adds to the decor. The cased heading provides a simple hanging mechanism.

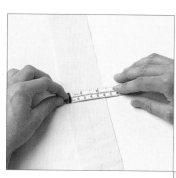

◄ STEP 1: TURN THE TOP
This cased heading has a self-frill that stands up above the curtain pole. To make the heading, fold a double hem that is deep enough to make both the slot for the pole and the frill. Pin two parallel seams to indicate the slot into which the curtain pole will comfortably fit.

STEP 2: TACK THE HEADING ►
Right Before you tack along the two seam lines, try the pole in the slot to check the fit. If the pole fits too tightly in the slot, the curtain will be difficult to draw. If there is too much slack fabric, the heading will not stand up neatly. Adjust the fit, if necessary.

◄ STEP 3: SEW THE SLOT
Machine stitch along the tacked seam lines, working in the same direction for both seams so that the fabric does not pucker. Take out the tacking stitches, and press the heading on the wrong side; if necessary, use a steam iron. Insert the pole, gathering up the curtain along it, and hang in place.

Artificial light

CLASSIC SOLUTION
A spotlight clipped to a shelf is a classic way to illuminate a small desk or work surface.

SUITED TO THE TASK
Below Recessed into the ceiling, these low-voltage halogen spots cast a crisp, bright light that is well suited to kitchen tasks.

ALTHOUGH IT WOULD be unhealthy to live in a world lit by halogen bulbs and fluorescent tubes, there is no denying that artificial light enables a room to function more efficiently than natural light alone allows.

The uniform intensity of artificial light can never be a substitute for the subtle shifts of natural light, yet modern lighting methods make it possible to control and modulate light in a room, and provide essential contrast and variety. It helps to suit the light to the purpose: use tungsten light for its warm glow, halogen light for its crispness, fluorescent light for its ability to illuminate without casting shadows. When daylight is limited, fit full-spectrum bulbs – which mimic natural daylight with their color balance – to guard against tiredness, lethargy, and "winter blues."

HOSPITABLE DINING
Right A decorative glass ceiling pendant provides background light so that diners feel and look their best. Mirrors reflect and multiply gently diffused candlelight, enhancing the opulent atmosphere.

MORE LIGHT
A broad beam of artificial light is set to focus where it is most needed.

DOUBLE DUTY
Far right This naturally dark, narrow hallway is fitted with broad-beam uplighters whose warm yellow glow illuminates the space and highlights the magnificent wooden beams set high above.

Let artificial

AMBIENT LIGHTING
Left A torchère gives ambient or background lighting. To keep this at a low level, fit dimmer switches to control and vary brightness.

TASK LIGHTING
Right Use small shaded lamps to focus light on the job in hand. Good clear light is especially important for reading.

ACCENT LIGHTING
Left Soft, warm-toned, low-level light from wall, table, or floor, is ideal for highlighting objects that are worthy of note, such as a favorite picture.

light be subtle rather than uniform in its intensity.

Pressed-flower candles

TIMELESS BEAUTY COMBINES with function in the simple form of candles. Their magic brings a room alive, or you can burn them outside, protected in containers and grouped together to make a decorative glow. These creamy candles preserve the flowers and leaves of summer, and are luxurious in a practical, simple way. Burning them releases the scent of the essential oil added to the dipping wax, enveloping the air with a delicious fragrance that can be as soothing or as uplifting as you wish (see Step 3). Set the candles in a suitable container, on plates or saucers, or just on a protected surface. Never leave them to burn unattended.

GROW a pot of chives and let them flower, then fill a jug with the airy blooms.

WHAT YOU NEED
PLAIN CANDLES
TISSUE PAPER, PRESSED PLANT MATERIAL
PARAFFIN WAX
HEATPROOF CONTAINER, SAUCEPAN
ESSENTIAL OIL
SMALL SPOON WITH HEATPROOF HANDLE
PLIERS
WIRE RACK

1 Take several thicknesses of acid-free tissue paper and lay them in strips on a work surface. Arrange the pressed flowers and leaves on the tissue-paper strips, and try out combinations of colors, textures, and forms until you are happy with the finished design.

3 Take the saucepan off the heat, but leave the container in the saucepan to keep the wax liquid and warm. Add a few drops of essential oil to the melted wax (suggestions: rose and lavender soothe; cedar and citrus uplift). The scent will be less strong when the wax cools and hardens.

5 Position the flower (or leaf) on the indented area of the candle, pressing gently but firmly to fix it in place. Reheat the bowl of the spoon and roll it gently over the flower (or leaf) to secure it. Repeat until the design is complete.

2 Place small chunks of the paraffin wax in a heatproof container, then place it in a saucepan half filled with simmering water. (Or use a heatproof bowl over a pan of simmering water). Set the pan over a gentle heat until the wax has completely melted.

4 Lay a cloth over the work surface. Warm the bowl of the spoon by holding it over a hotplate or gas burner. Take one of the plain candles, and press the bowl of the spoon against its side so that the wax softens and an indent forms into which the first flower (or leaf) will fit.

6 To seal the design, dip the candle in melted wax, prepared in Step 3. Use pliers to firmly grasp the candle by its wick, and then immerse the candle in the wax for about three seconds to coat the design. Place the candle on a wire rack. Let the wax coating dry for at least one hour before burning the candle.

Combining light

LETTING GO
Above By day or night, a satisfying union of ivory candles and soft, modern lighting creates a setting that soothes and relaxes.

THREE IN ONE
Right A restful bedroom makes good use of light from different sources. Wall-to-wall windows let in plenty of natural light, halogen ceiling spots on dimmer switches can be adjusted for varied levels of background light, and a tall shaded table lamp spreads out warm light for bedtime reading.

NEVER FORGET THAT poor lighting can mar the most beautifully decorated room, and not only that, it can make you feel positively ill at ease. To function well, a lighting plan should be a happy balance of controlled natural light and sympathetic artificial light that takes account of different activities, and varies the amount and quality of light accordingly.

Clear, direct light is absolutely essential in kitchens, bathrooms, hallways, and on stairways, both for safety and comfortable movement at night; add task lighting where close work, such as food preparation, demands it. Set a quieter mood in sitting rooms and bedrooms with filmy curtains or translucent blinds to filter harsh natural light, and introduce diffused light from table, floor, or wall lamps rather than ceiling pendants.

Good lighting

HAPPY HOUR
Right This room is made to welcome evening ease. At dusk, wide French doors and long walls of windows admit what is left of the natural light, which is supplemented with twinkling candles and a glowing oil lamp.

FLEXIBLE FRIEND
Below A lightweight floor lamp can be moved from place to place as needed, offering flexible lighting options for varied needs.

FINE TUNING
The lamp can be adjusted for both height and angle.

SMART TRICKS

• To open up small rooms, reflect light onto the ceiling with torchères. Use wall-mounted models to save space.

• To focus a broad beam of light onto a work surface, use fish-eye spotlights.

• To fill a room with discreet background light, fit low-voltage spotlights, recessed into the ceiling, on dimmer switches.

LIGHT REFRESHMENT
Left In a multifunctional space, an area dedicated to dining enjoys natural light from the windows on one side of the table. The low ceiling pendant directs intimate, golden light onto the table itself.

HIDDEN ASSETS
Right A quirky bathroom is furnished with unusual wall sconces as task lights on either side of the two mirrors. Above eye level, uplighters are a hidden source of ambient light.

is absolutely essential for both safety and comfort.

Polka dot lampshade

USING OLD toothbrushes is thrifty, and they are just the tool for this project.

GOOD LIGHTING is an essential part of creating a comfortable home, and it is very satisfying to customize an inexpensive fabric lampshade to blend with a color scheme or brighten a plain room. You can add a personal, distinctive touch with a beaded or tasseled trim, or by embellishing the lampshade with pastel chalks or felt pens. The oil-paint sticks used here transform the entire surface of the shade with broad stripes and polka dots of intense color; the sticks are easy to use and give a professional finish. Begin with this graphic design, which is simplicity itself. Then let your horizons expand to fill your imagination.

WHAT YOU NEED

PLAIN FABRIC LAMPSHADE

DUSTSHEET OR LARGE OLD SHEET

SOFT LEAD PENCIL

OIL-PAINT STICKS (FROM ART SHOPS)

CLEAN OLD TOOTHBRUSHES

LINT-FREE SOFT CLOTHS OR KITCHEN PAPER

1 Choose any lampshade in a plain, neutral fabric, such as unbleached cotton (the finished shade is safe to use with a standard light bulb). Lay the sheet over the work surface to keep it clean. Draw lines on the outside of the lampshade with the pencil, indicating the segments of colors in the design.

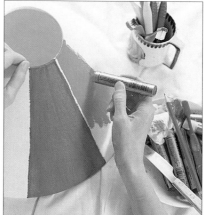

2 Use the oil-paint sticks to fill in segments of color. Leave a thin strip of fabric uncolored between each segment to enhance the graphic effect, if liked. Work your way around the shade counterclockwise if you are right-handed, and clockwise if you are left-handed. This prevents your working hand from rubbing against the color as you finish each segment.

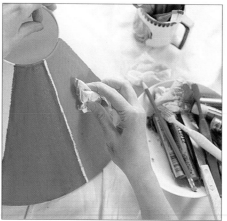

3 When all the segments are filled in, rub the oil paint into the fabric using a clean, dry, old toothbrush for each different color. Use a circular motion to work the paint thoroughly into the fabric. Work, segment by segment, counterclockwise or clockwise, as in Step 2.

4 When you have finished rubbing the paint into all of the segments, use a lint-free, soft cloth or wad of kitchen paper to gently remove any oil paint remaining on the surface of the fabric. Use a different wad for each color. Let the lampshade dry in a warm place overnight.

5 When the base colors are dry, you may like to enhance the design with polka dots, as here. To do this, use the same oil paint sticks to apply rough blobs of contrasting colors on top of the base colors. Let the shade dry again in a warm place overnight before use.

Color

Thinking about color

MOST OF US RECOGNIZE up to two hundred colors, although we do not all view them in the same way: ask any two people to describe any color, and you will probably receive two very different responses. Some cultures, such as the Maoris of New Zealand, have many words to describe a single color: in tune with nature, they have myriad words to describe the different reds of fruits and flowers. Other languages, such as ancient Greek, have few words for color, in spite of developing out of a culture renowned for its scholars, philosophers, and intellectual debate.

Scientists have long known that color affects mood and emotion. At the turn of the twentieth century, the Swiss psychologist, Carl Jung, wrote: *Colors are the mother tongue of the subconscious*. Color can evoke long-forgotten recollections and sensations. Never ignore your emotional response to color, because positive associations can enhance your sense of well-being.

When choosing colors for your home, you could begin with a treasured possession or an object that pleases you, and plan the color scheme for a room around it. Alternatively, collect samples and images

Bring hither the pink and purple columbine, with

that inspire or excite you. Test a patch of paint on a wall, and pin large swatches of fabric at a window or onto furniture. View them at various times of day over a period of several days, observing the changes that occur in different light and weather conditions.

Consider the conventions of using color, but be ready to disregard them if you choose. For example, small spaces appear larger when decorated with pale colors or neutral shades. Instead, create a room of uplifting, jewel-like brilliance to compensate for lack of space. A range of tones in a single color palette,

for example, taupe, donkey, and charcoal gray, is naturally appealing, harmonious, and comfortable to the eye. Color contrasts such as red and green reverberate against each other, and create a lively, invigorating effect. If you do not wish to redecorate, use soft furnishings to add splashes of color. This is an easy and inexpensive way to revitalize a room.

Nature is full of color. Take a walk in the park, spend an afternoon in the flower garden, or watch the sun going down to gain wonderful inspiration. Relish color, and luxuriate in it for its tonic effect.

gillyflowers, cowslips, kingcups, and loved lilies.
Edmund Spenser

The decorator's color wheel

UNDERSTANDING THE THEORY of color is greatly simplified when basic colors, and combinations of them, are represented as a traditional color wheel. Even if the decorator's needs differ from those of the artist, this tool will help you to become familiar with common terms that interior designers (as well as artists) apply to color and its use.

The color wheel illustrated here identifies the three *primary* colors – red, yellow, blue – and the three *secondary* colors – orange, green, purple. It is easy to see that each color has unique properties. The colors known as *complementary pairs* are those that lie directly opposite each other – red–green, orange–blue, yellow–purple. Each pair has a perfect balance that feels "just right." Finally, the colors that lie next to each other are known as *harmonies*.

THE PRIMARY COLORS

Below The three primary colors are red, yellow, and blue. They are called "primary" because they exist in their own right; they cannot be reproduced by mixing other colors. To soften the effect of these pure, clear colors, mix them with white, gray, or neutral tones.

RED
This bold, warm color is guaranteed to create an impact wherever you use it, since it stimulates both mind and body.

YELLOW
The warmth, energy, and life-enhancing properties of the sun are embodied in yellow. Use this color to stir happy emotions.

BLUE
Perceived as the color of the intellect, blue conjures up visions of sky and sea. It has an expansive quality that calms and soothes.

THE COMPLEMENTARY PAIRS

Below One primary and one secondary color makes up each of these three pairs. Lying opposite each other, the colors are not only complementary, but play off one another, producing vibrant effects.

RED–GREEN
This dynamic and startling combination highlights the stimulating effect of red. It is supported by green's almost squeaky clarity.

BLUE–ORANGE
In this pairing, the intense drama of orange is offset by the soothing quality of blue – yet the orange still retains its vibrancy.

YELLOW–PURPLE
There can be an irritable edge to purple. Cheerful, uncomplicated yellow is the ideal partner to lift and brighten the mood.

Use the color wheel and consider the conventions, if you wish, but be prepared to disregard them too.

THE SECONDARY COLORS

Below The three secondary colors lie between pairs of primary colors, and are made by mixing equal quantities of the pairs: red and yellow to make orange, yellow and blue to make green, blue and red to make purple. Use secondary colors to extend the scope of the primaries.

ORANGE
Cosy and inviting, orange can also overwhelm with its intensity. It is easier to use when softened into tones such as apricot.

GREEN
Harmony, balance, and regeneration reign with green: its qualities reflect nature's own. Use it to give new life to a room.

PURPLE
The depth and richness of purple can sometimes be overwhelming. Relieve its oppressive tendency with sunny orange or yellow.

Primary colors

IN YOUR HOME, as in life, color speaks all languages. It brings vitality to any space, be it a period dwelling or a modern home, and plays tricks with senses and mind to make a room feel warm or cool, or appear larger or smaller than it really is.

Used together, the primary colors of red, yellow, and blue combine in a gloriously bold celebration of life. Such decisive use of color is not to everyone's taste, especially in bedrooms that are traditionally decked out in tones or shades of color that are (at the very least) quieter. There is no doubt that strong colors and contrasts create immense visual energy. Some might say, however, that they are made for a bedroom setting, guaranteeing a vibrant start to the day and an uplifting mood at the end.

YELLOW WITH RED
Painted egg-yolk yellow, the window recesses sing out jubilantly against the intense magenta of the diaphanous embroidered roman blinds. Their delicate fabric filters bright sunlight and turns it into a rosy glow.

VALUED POSSESSIONS CONFIRM THE COLOR THEME
The feast of bold color in this room is united in an accumulation of possessions. Pottery, prints, paintings, rugs, books, lamps, strings of beads – in fact, every decorative element, including the radiator covers, adds considered but unselfconscious texture to the theme.

SHAPES & COLORS
A beaded textile laid across the seat of an old oak chair contains variations of all the colors seen in the room. Its rectangles and triangles echo the larger blocks of color on the bedspread and walls.

Be as Bold & Daring as you Like

In this electrifying bedroom, cushions, throws, paint, and art objects in tones of the three primary colors are combined with skill into a harmonious whole. If you do not fancy strong color, you can introduce a multicolored element simply with a posy of flowers.

START SMALL, THINK BIG
A posy of ranunculus might have been the starting point for this ambitious scheme. Mix and match colors and textures, and live with them for a while to feel the effect. Texture is important to add the tonal variety that brings color to life.

DEPTH & TEXTURE
Egg-yolk yellow runs as a continuous motif around the whole room on the woodwork of cupboard doors, skirtings, and door and window moldings. Brush marks are retained rather than painted out to create a striated effect.

MUTED TONES
The multilayered theme is repeated in small and large rugs that lie over each other. Their softness and muted tones provide a visual relief from the strong colors.

Red

PLANTS, TREES, AND insect once provided the pigments for dye, and their names have passed into general use to become the common language of color. Today, as then, madder describes red-purple, annatto is a yellowish red, and cochineal the vivid red we call crimson.

In nature, red highlights poisonous berries and deadly fungi: it is a color to stop you in your tracks. At home, you can use accents of red in a similar way, as decorative punctuation marks that call attention to an architectural feature or object. Remember its associations, and use the color accordingly. In China, it spells luck and happiness, in India, marriage – and universally, romance. Red light excites the brain, so red arouses passions. Pink is gentler, the color of girl babies, because – as one legend would have it – they were born inside pale pink roses.

ENTERTAIN WITH A SWING
Right Choose red where the intention is to stimulate the mind and excite the senses, as in rooms for entertaining. Its boldness copes well with wood and burnished leather.

LIVELY EXCHANGE
Below left Tomato red above mellow pine paneling gives this small study a cozy feel, and encourages productive work. The blue of the chair is a pleasant color contrast.

SHOCKING PINK
Below Transformed into shocking pink, red is given a modern twist ideally suited to a white space. Here, it is anchored against turquoise, delineated with jet black.

People hesitate before using red, but to disregard it

is to miss the cheer and energy it brings to a room.

Glazed & textured wall

THE SIMPLEST decoration is often the most effective too, and this cross-hatched wall treatment is no exception. Separate layers of translucent paint, or glaze, are used to achieve the subtle color and texture. Each layer modifies the tone of the color beneath while preserving and adding depth to the textured pattern. You can dilute colored emulsion paint for the water-based glaze, or tint white emulsion with pigment (see Step 1) to get your color choice. The absorbency of the wall material will determine the consistency of the glaze, but it must not be so diluted that it runs when applied. Try it, mistakes can always be painted over.

A STACK of plain, checked, and patterned fabrics is a fine source of inspiration.

WHAT YOU NEED

WHITE EMULSION PAINT & PIGMENT OF CHOICE (SEE STEP 1)

SUGAR SOAP (SEE STEP 3, FROM DIY SHOPS)

7IN (18CM) OR 9IN (22CM) PAINT ROLLER, DEPENDING ON AREA TO BE COVERED

4IN (10CM) PAINTBRUSH WITH COARSE BRISTLES

1 You can use colored emulsion paint, diluted with water to make a thin translucent glaze, but it is far more fun to make your own glaze by tinting white emulsion with pigment in the form of either artist's acrylics (in tubes), universal stainers (in plastic bottles), or powder pigments (in packets). The subtle tones of powder pigments seem best suited to this project.

2 Make sure the room you are working in is well ventilated, and wear a dust mask. Dilute the white emulsion paint with water; stop when it is a bit thicker than desired. Dissolve a teaspoonful of the powder pigment in a small amount of water, add to the paint, and mix well. To adjust the color, add more pigment, paint, or water, but do not make the glaze too runny.

3 To prepare a plain plaster wall, whisk away dust with a soft-bristled brush. To prepare a painted wall, wash with a solution of sugar soap (follow the directions on the packet), rinse well, and leave to dry. Use a roller to apply the base coat of glaze, and leave to dry overnight.

4 When the base coat of glaze is completely dry, use the paintbrush to apply a second coat. Work on a small area at a time, dragging the paintbrush vertically with continuous light strokes. The base coat should show through the dragged second coat. Leave to dry overnight.

5 Use the paintbrush to drag a third coat of glaze horizontally across the second, again using continuous light strokes; this creates the cross-hatched pattern. Leave to dry overnight. The sealed, hard-wearing surface that the glaze provides can be wiped clean with a damp cloth.

Blue

WHEN THE SKY is blue, life seems better and your spirits rise – but why is that? Perhaps the comfort you get with blue comes from its being associated with infinity and eternity – the expanse of the universe, the ebb and flow of tides – that is so reassuring in a world of change.

It is said that after an operation to remove a cataract from his eye, the great landscape artist, Claude Monet, was amazed by all the blueness in the world. Blue varies enormously. At one end of the tonal spectrum it is navy, passing by way of indigo (the velvety purplish-blue that was once obtained from woad) and cornflower to the ice-blue of white diamonds. Whatever shade of blue you choose, you can rely on it to be cool, calm, and collected. Note, however, that the paler shades are uncomfortable in low light, where their austerity can appear cold.

TRANQUIL SYMMETRY
Left The combination of blue and white gives this tastefully furnished room a simple charm. The furniture is placed in a symmetrical group to underline the calm quality of the colors.

DECORATIVE DETAILS
Soft blue walls pick up a suggestion of green in the bedlinen, and provide a pleasing backdrop to the intense saturated color of a painted canvas.

GINGHAM BEDROOM
Right Woven gingham is a classic favorite for informal rooms, where its understated elegance works particularly well. In this check, blue veers towards sea green. The red-striped bolsters are an inspired bit of zing.

REFRESHING CHANGE
Left Too often floors are just a neutral backdrop. The gleaming sapphire floor of this streamlined kitchen, offset by white walls, white appliances, and chrome shelving, is a refreshing, functional change from the norm.

CLEAN & FRESH
Right If pure blue is too much for your taste, try blue-greens, which have a lighter touch and add balance. The colors of this futuristic bathroom, dominated by a cedar tub, recall a moist cave.

REFLECTED INTEREST
These glossy walls glow and twinkle with reflected light, adding depth and interest to a monochrome scheme.

Blues and whites are perfect together. Consider willow-patterned china or the freshness of homespun gingham checks.

Yellow

IT IS RECORDED that yellow was the favored color of the philosophers, Confucius and Socrates, for it stimulates and inspires. Most cultures associate yellow with the sun, and thus with warmth and energy. Yellow, in its pure, clear, primary form, was unknown outside nature before the manufacture of chrome yellow at the beginning of the nineteenth century: earlier yellows were muted, and obtained from ocher and raw sienna.

Every room benefits from a touch of yellow to bring out its flavor, in the same way that salt brings out the flavor of food. Yellow drenches a room with light when the sun shines, and makes a room glow on dull days, or where there are few or no windows – for example, in an enclosed bathroom. Yellow brings a ray of sunshine to the smallest space, and looks well in artificial light, too.

Every room benefits from a touch of yellow to

SOFTER OPTION
Left If this is your first go with yellow, it is safer to opt for the softer end of its spectrum. Creams and pale yellows are easy to use, positive without being insistent, and will enliven and brighten any room, especially when used with muted pinks and blues.

MOVABLE COLOR
Right Yellow works as well on furniture as on walls. The strong blocks of saturated color on this folding screen buzz and reverberate with vibrant energy, yet look fresh and modern with the white of the walls, floor, and furnishings.

COZY COMBINATION
Left Yellow provides a good background for a range of other colors. Warm reds, oranges, and purples used with yellow make this drawing room intimate and welcoming.

BRIGHT STAIRWAY
Below left Strong color works well in spaces that are used frequently but for only a few minutes at a time. This stairwell is aglow with deep yellow walls that tone with the mellowness of wood.

FRESH ACCENTS
Below Acid yellows, for all their freshness, can be uncomfortable and even cold to live with. Here, whitewashed walls and woodwork, and neutral tones, relieve and soften the sharp edge of yellow.

bring out its flavor, just as salt does with food.

Patchwork curtain

THE HOMESPUN simplicity of patchwork is enhanced by plain fabrics in bold colors.

MUCH OF THE JOY of patchwork is in piecing together a unique pattern out of bits of colored fabric, often at very little cost. It is particularly appropriate for the theme of well-being at home that the square (the traditional patchwork template) symbolizes not only abundance and achievement but order and balance too. The success of patchwork depends on the interest and rhythm of the pattern and the inherent charm of the fabrics. Scraps from a ragbag or pieces of worn-out clothing, beloved and with many a cherished memory, add to its appeal. Stitch patchwork by hand, or by machine; a large door curtain may need several sittings.

<table>
<tr><td>

WHAT YOU NEED

RAGBAG SCRAPS OR FIRM-WEAVE FABRIC

NEEDLE & THREAD

DRESSMAKER'S PINS

PINKING SHEARS

PLAIN LINING FABRIC

BRASS CURTAIN RINGS WITH EYELETS

EMBROIDERY THREAD

WOOD OR METAL CURTAIN POLE

</td></tr>
</table>

1 If you are using scraps, try to choose fabrics of roughly similar weights, for example, cotton and linen, not linen and voile. Wash and iron the pieces before use, if necessary. Cut the fabric into large and small squares: good sizes are 6in (15cm) and 4in (10cm). Hand-sew the smaller squares to the large ones; use contrasting thread and small, even running stitches.

2 Make as many double squares as you need; if you like, fringe some of the small squares on the edges before sewing them to the large squares. To make the curtain, turn a narrow hem along all four edges of the large squares and press flat. Matching the right sides of the hems, pin two squares together. Oversew by hand to join them. Repeat for all the patchwork squares.

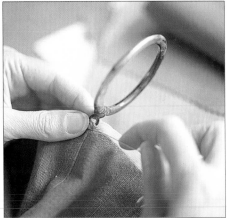

3 Use pinking shears to cut four fabric strips, 2in (5cm) wide, for the four edges of the curtain. Fold one strip lengthwise, wrong sides together. Pin to the wrong side of the curtain and sew in place with the folded edge of the strip showing at the side. Do the other edges.

4 For the two long edges of the curtain, cut strips of fabric 1in (2.5cm) wide, and fringe down one long edge; a variety of colors gives an attractive finish. Pin to the wrong side of the curtain, and hand-sew neatly on the wrong side so that the stitching is invisible on the front.

5 Cut plain lining fabric a little larger than the curtain. Turn a narrow hem along the four edges; press flat. Pin, then hand-sew the lining to the wrong side of the curtain. Use embroidery thread to oversew the eyelet rings to the top of the curtain, then hang it from a heavy pole.

Changing the pace

COLOR CAN MODIFY your perception of space and light, and may be used to suggest heat or cold, space or intimacy. The most subtle change of hue will make a room seem a little warmer or a bit more spacious, by degrees. Anyone can transform a cheerless room into a joyous celebration of color, creating happy clashes and brightness to make the heart miss a beat.

Light colors and neutral shades appear to enlarge small spaces, while warm reds, yellows, and oranges create rooms that are intimate and welcoming. Strong color is intensified and becomes richer when levels of natural light are low. Space is brought to life with contrasting color and highlights, which can be as simple as moldings painted to emphasize the detail.

SMALL-SPACE DRAMA
A tiny vestibule provides a dramatic demonstration of the power of color to transform space. Light and dark checks confuse and amuse the eye into forgetting the restricted dimensions of this hall.

PERCEPTION OF COLOR
Painted the same color as the wall at right angles to it, this surface appears darker because it receives less natural light.

RED OVER ALL
Below right This lofty room has the cheerful energy that only red can achieve. Its grand proportions have been controlled by washing the same color over the ceiling and walls.

ALL-WHITE ROOM
White paintwork reflects all the available light and gives an illusion of greater space. Brilliant white can be cold, but pure white (like sunshine) enhances and complements color throughout the spectrum, making it seem more luminous and crisp.

TRANSFORM YOUR HOME

Pale colors and neutral shades appear to open up small rooms, and transform those with little natural light into bright spaces. Dark colors enclose rooms and make them cozy. Use color to manipulate the quality of your environment and the energy in your home, to make extraordinary an ordinary space.

GREEN CEILING & DADO
Color contrast on ceiling and walls, or walls and floor, adds interest to a room and helps to avoid blandness. A darker color visually lowers an uncomfortably high ceiling. Strong, saturated color enriches a room, and distracts attention from defects.

INTIMATE DINING
Left Yellow stimulates, inspires, and recalls the sun, so every room can do with a bit of it. This somber dining corner has vibrant yellow walls and yellow ocher ceiling that transform it into a lively, glowing space.

EXPANDED SPACE
Below Pale, subtly varied neutral shades emphasize the airy spaciousness of rooms that enjoy much light. Paint looks darker on flat or matte surfaces than on shiny or glossy ones, which naturally reflect more light.

Secondary colors

BY MIXING TWO or more of the primary colors (red, yellow, and blue), all other colors can be made. The secondary colors are made by mixing together equal quantities of the two primary colors that lie on either side of them on the color wheel (see pages 68–69); so (in a clockwise direction), orange is made from red and yellow, green is made from yellow and blue, and purple is made from blue and red.

The secondaries extend your choice of colors and are therefore very important in the decoration of your home. Perhaps the color most frequently used is green, and you should try to have something green in every space (even if only a potted plant or a bunch of leaves) for its many associations with nature. After all, green is the color of spring, of renewal and fresh growth. Use it to rejuvenate any corner of a room.

CONTEMPORARY CHIC
Orange goes with most purples. Here, a stylized contemporary interior is enlivened with splashes of both, turning it into a celebration of color.

ALL THREE TOGETHER
Right A combination of purple, orange, and green as pure hues would be overpowering. Instead, in this much-used kitchen, muted tones of the three secondaries are entirely complementary. On the dresser, purple has been color washed with blue for a layered effect.

DECORATIVE ACCESSORIES
Interesting plates and bowls introduce personality as well as color into this scheme.

Two primary colors are mixed in equal parts to

ENVELOPING WALLS
Wrap a room in a harmony of color. Apply it to walls, floors, and ceilings alike.

BEDROOM HARMONY
Right Most greens are an effortless harmony. Easy on the eye, green is an accommodating, versatile color. Take inspiration from nature's hues (peas in their pods, shiny acid green apples), and match vivid limes with flashes of fuchsia or orange.

make the secondaries: orange, green, and purple.

SOFT SHADES
Choose muted tones for an interesting rather than hectic effect in enclosed spaces.

COLOR AS IT IS

• Paint a reasonable area of a wall to see what a color will look like in a room: it is hard to tell from sample swatches.

• Look at color in natural and artificial light. It will appear different in both.

• Experiment with ideas in rooms that are less often used.

TONIC EFFECT
Above Here is brightness to make the heart miss a beat, a room of uplifting jewel-like brilliance in which orange and vivid pink bring the space to life. Luxuriate in color, with contrasts, highlights, and happy clashes, and value it as a tonic.

FALL SQUARES
Left Butted together to suggest tiled walls, these harmonious squares of color recall those of fall leaves. Faded versions of the secondary hues are naturally comfortable to the eye – a visual relief from strong, pure color.

Green

THE PRIMARIES, blue and yellow, make green, which is one of the three secondary colors. Traditionally, green represents balance and harmony. It is the color of the landscape, reminiscent of fresh growth and symbolic of the natural cycle of birth, life, and death.

We acknowledge and mark this natural association of green with prosaic, down-to-earth names for different shades of the color, among them olive, mint, pea, and lime. From an early age, our sense of color is learned from the landscape, and color associations that occur in the natural world suggest combinations to use at home. Most greens harmonize effortlessly, as they do in nature. Consider the wealth of greens in fruits and vegetables alone – tart apples, avocados, crinkled cabbages – and team them with any other hue to glorious effect.

DARING CHOICE
Left To use bold color in a tiny bedroom may seem overly daring, but it counterbalances the huge bed, which might otherwise dominate the entire space.

MOSTLY WHITE
Right A predominantly white, spacious seating area is enlivened and made more friendly by the addition of vivid green scatter cushions, lampshade, and loose cover for an easy chair.

Easy on the eye and soothing too, green is a valuable color in any room where fine work is done.

ECHOES OF COLOR
Above The white china and bubbly blue-green recycled glass, displayed on open dresser shelves, echo the fresh colors of crisp gingham that hides less decorative kitchen accessories below.

DARK TO LIGHT
Below With their color wash of buttery yellow, these walls make a good background for intensely deep green woodwork, and bring much-needed light to a dark passage and twisting stairway.

Homegrown milk paint

RECYCLE a milk carton as a decorative container for paintbrushes and pencils.

THERE IS GROWING INTEREST in paint that is pleasant and safe to use, made from natural, readily available ingredients. Milk paint has been used since ancient times, but it is most associated with colonial America. Then, oil paint was a luxury, the components expensive and hard to obtain, but it was simple to produce milk paints and water-based paints at home. Milk paint is especially suitable for wood, but can be used on any interior surface, and has no smell once dry. The finish is durable, and can be wiped clean with a damp cloth. Mix up the paint in small, manageable quantities: slight variations in color add character to the effect.

1 Prepare the milk for the paint at least one week before you want to use it; a clear container will allow you to check the progress of the separating milk. Pour the skim milk into the container, and cover with a cloth. Put the container in a warm place and leave for about seven days, or until the milk has separated into solid curds and liquid whey.

2 Put the sieve over a bowl, pour off the whey, and discard it. Use the spoon to press the curd through the sieve into the bowl. Leave to stand for a few hours, then drain off and discard any whey left in the bowl. Prepare the surface to be decorated – an unpainted one needs no priming. All surfaces should be lightly sanded. Afterwards, brush off any debris.

3 Color the curd with water-based pigment, such as universal stainers, using one color or mixing them to create a color of your choice, as here. Use a teaspoon to measure out the pigment, and note the proportions for reference. Test the mix on a piece of white card; remember that the color of the dried paint will be less intense. Finally, mix the pigment into the curd until well blended; the resulting paint will be pastelike and quite thick.

4 Apply the paint with a paintbrush. Work it well into the wood, and follow the direction of its grain; the wood may show through this first coat. Let it dry overnight, then apply a second coat of paint, and let this dry again overnight. To finish, use a clean soft cloth to apply one coat of beeswax polish (see page 140), rubbing it well into the grain of the wood.

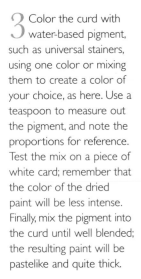

Orange

WHEN A PRISM splits light into the rainbow of colors, orange comes between red and yellow – and it is indeed a mix of these two colors. More gentle than yellow or red, orange works in harmony with both, and is always welcoming and suggestive of intimacy.

In Japan and China, orange is the color of love and happiness. The citron is one of the three blessed fruits of the Buddha, and an orange lotus flower symbolizes the Sanskrit word for *one's abode*. In the north-eastern United States and China, "leafers" travel great distances to revel in dazzling fall color as leaves change from sharp orange through gold and russet before falling. Flickering flames are orange, and orange is a revitalizing reminder of the visual stimulus of sunset and sunrise, for to watch the sun rise and set is always an exhilarating experience.

WELCOME ENTRANCE
Left Myriad tones are encompassed in orange, from apricot to mellow terra-cotta. The glow in this entrance hall recalls the subdued shades of the earth pigments that were once used to color water-based paints.

MELLOW WOOD
A staircase with treads polished smooth by time is a perfect complement to the muted tones of color washed walls.

ORANGE WITH BLUE
Right An intimate space for comfortable dining resonates with a clear orange – a fashionable Art Deco shade. It pairs well with adjacent walls of strongly contrasting cool greenish-blue.

SINK INTO COMFORT
Left Terra-cotta means, literally, *baked earth*. This deepest of oranges may lack the brilliance, fire, and vibrancy of primary red or yellow, but its soft warmth makes it an easy, comfortable color to be with, day-in and day-out.

GLOWING LAMP
In keeping with the color choice for this room, the lighting is at once intimate and restrained. The light of the lamp is diffused with a thick parchment shade.

FLATTERING GLOW
Below The warm glow reflected by these boldly patterned terra-cotta walls is very flattering. It is an especially welcome color in rooms that are naturally cold or starved of sun, tinting light that is reminiscent of golden summer evenings.

Purple

THE RANGE OF HUES between red and blue is gathered together in purple, including soft tones of lavender, lilac, mauve, and violet. Deep purple is a sign of royalty and priestly power, is a ceremonial color for formal rooms, and traditionally denotes *the love of truth and the truth of love.* In accordance with the language of flowers, violets are the emblem of innocence.

Since ancient times, fabric dyes been obtained from lichens growing along the Mediterranean coast that yield beautiful, light-sensitive shades from the deepest purple through to amethyst and violet. In decorating your home, the pale purple shade of lavender may be the easiest in this tonal range to use. It is as charming and countrified as its name suggests, and brings a breath of freshness to a room when combined with white or green.

Traditionally, purple denotes "the love of truth...the truth of love."

TRANQUIL BEDROOM
Left Pale, restful tones of purple are the most suitable for peaceful, personal rooms, such as bedrooms and studies. In this Swedish house, rag rugs striped yellow and mauve soften the limed floorboards.

LOFTY BATHROOM
Right Mixed with purple, blue becomes lavender. These shades are deftly combined in a geometric border of ceramic tiles, set against gently color washed walls to create a bathroom that is at once dramatic and restful.

SHEER EXTRAVAGANCE
Above Those inclined to
flamboyance might coat
a room in the purple of
sugared almonds, which
makes a fitting backdrop
for the candy-striped sofa,
venetian blinds, and crisp
white bedlinens here.

PASTEL ACCENTS
Below Painted in lozenge
shades of tangerine, lilac,
lemon, and plum, these
decoratively curvaceous
chairs provide delightful
pools of silky-soft color
in a space that is in other
ways carefully neutral.

Basket-weave ribbon cushion

BE AS cautious or as daring as you like with your choice of cushion ribbons.

A GOOD WAY to start using color – especially if you feel unsure about it – is in decorative accessories, such as this cushion. For its woven front, cotton ribbons in varying widths and bright colors are crossed to form a simple pattern. The pattern is complicated and embellished by sewing flat zigzag braid, known as rickrack, onto some of the ribbons. Choose two colors to make a simple check, or dazzle and delight the senses with a celebration of many vibrant shades of sumptuous silk velvet or satin ribbon. Alternatively, make the cushion in a single color, and transform it into something that can be enjoyed for its texture alone.

WHAT YOU NEED

SQUARE CUSHION PAD

FABRIC, SUCH AS CANVAS OR TICKING, FOR CUSHION COVER

RIBBONS & FLAT ZIGZAG BRAID

DRESSMAKER'S PINS

NEEDLE & THREAD

BIAS BINDING 2IN (5CM) WIDE

PIPING CORD

1 Lay the cushion pad on the fabric, and cut out two pieces that are a little larger all around than the pad. Set one piece aside. Lay the ribbons and braid on the other piece; cut to the same size. Pin, tack, and machine stitch the braid to some of the ribbons. Make a second set in the same way. Pin, tack, and machine stitch one set to the fabric at top and bottom only.

2 To weave the pattern, take one ribbon from the second set, and lay it at right angles to the first set; pin at the left-hand side to secure. Weave the ribbon under and then over the vertical ribbons, then pin it in place on the right-hand side. Align the next ribbon underneath, and repeat the weaving process. Weave in all of the ribbons until the pattern is complete.

3 Tack the second (horizontally placed) set of ribbons in place on the left- and right-hand sides of the fabric, then machine stitch in place. The ribbons should form a tight weave. Make a small hand-stitch here and there through to the back of the fabric to secure them, if necessary.

4 For the piping, cut a length of bias binding to fit around the cover, plus a little extra for overlap. Cut the piping cord to the same length. Enclose the cord in the binding (right side out), pinning close to the cord as you go. Tack close to the cord, then remove the pins.

5 Tack the piping all around the edge of the ribbon-covered fabric. With right sides facing, pin the two square fabric pieces together on three sides; tack, then machine stitch. Turn the cover right sides out. Insert the cushion pad, then close the opening with neat slip-stitches.

Two-color painting

BY USING MORE than one color in a room, you can transform it to abound with vibrant light, and create color schemes to evoke any mood. First paint the ceiling, to avoid splashing freshly painted walls, then tackle the difficult bits. Cut in (that is, neatly paint) the junction where wall and ceiling meet. Next do woodwork and walls, ensuring clean lines between the two. Cutting in is not difficult. A steady hand, a full paintbrush, and a little confidence are all that is needed, and clearly defined lines between different surfaces will give a professional finish to your work.

◄ STEP 1: WALL & CEILING
Bring a loaded paintbrush parallel to, but a short distance from, the ceiling line. Be sure to apply more paint than if you were painting the full surface of the open wall.

STEP 2: WALL & CEILING ▶
Right Spread the paint upward into the junction of the wall and the ceiling. Make a straight line, using the outer bristles to bead paint into the junction.

◄ STEP 1: WALL & FRAME
Paint a series of small strips on the wall at right angles to the door or window frame, working from the frame outward.

STEP 2: WALL & FRAME ▶
Join the small strips with a steady line parallel to the frame. Ease the bristles close to the frame to make a defined edge. Do this throughout the room before painting the walls.

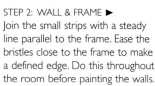

White

AT ONCE ORDINARY and dynamic, white is the symbol of purity. In color terms, it is the absence of pigment, but contains all the colors of the rainbow. In textile dyeing, white is achievable only by bleaching, thus providing the clean background needed for a pure pale color.

White rooms are cool and calm. Space seems enlarged with white, and daylight is emphasized, since white alone reflects surrounding light, bouncing it back into a room. White is a natural foil for almost any other hue or shade, adding sparkle and freshness. Dirty whites – for example, the beautiful mellow colors of whitewash – age well, and complement the faded character of worn wood and old fabric: use matte emulsion to simulate an aged patina on walls. Bright white suggests modernity, but there is a whole range of whites to suit the period home as well.

GLASS & STEEL
Right In this functional kitchen, light-reflecting white envelops the room, for it is applied to all surfaces and objects (except for the table), transforming a small area into a calm, efficient space.

HOMEY SETTING
Below left A harmony of whites creates a contemplative fireside corner. Boldly framed mirrors add textural interest and variety, which benefit all-white schemes.

BEDROOM TO DREAM IN
Below All blues look fresh and pretty with white. The peaceful aspect of this bedroom and its personal quality are enhanced by highlighting architectural details in lavender blue.

White encompasses myriad tones, from eggshell

to powdery stucco, bone, and bleached canvas.

Gray & black

CLOSELY RELATED TO white, gray comes in many subtly different shades that create a relaxing and contemplative atmosphere – but it is possible to achieve great liveliness and variety with muted grays and whites. For example, the blue-grays associated with the Gustavian period of eighteenth-century Sweden were greatly liked for their ability to enhance natural light and brighten rooms, so helping to dispel the gloom of long winters.

Black – the dramatic opposite of white – is its natural partner. Just as whites encompass a vast range of hues, so black describes tones from the blue-black of a midnight sky to the coppery gleam of ancient textiles. Juxtaposing black with white is a classic combination much favored by modernists, and a nostalgic reminder of lace collars on velvet dresses and checkered marble floors.

A spot of white instantly softens and civilizes black into gray...

PURPOSEFUL KITCHEN
Left A gray granite work surface and white metal accessories bring life to a small breakfast bar. Tiny amounts of black define the color scheme, and the waxed wooden floor sings against crisp white cabinets and paintwork.

GENTLEMAN'S ROOM
Right Here is proof that gray has sophistication. A fine contrast between charcoal gray walls and furnishings and a honey floorcovering transcends blandness in a pairing that has graphic appeal and is in no way dull.

LIFT THE MOOD
Above The understated
elegance of classic woven
checks brings a dynamic
touch to a simple, fresh
color scheme of sludgy
olive gray-green, warm
red, and white, blended
with purple and blue.

UNUSUAL MATERIAL
Below The soft gray of
natural concrete around
the bathtub reflects the
green tiles used within it,
and for the shower tray
beyond. A pink mat and
blue director's chair lift
the monochrome effect.

Glass bead door curtain

CHOOSE your beads with care: you will need dozens to make a large curtain.

THE OLD ADAGE that *blue and green should never be seen* is not upheld in the natural world, where these colors are seen in abundance together. Color is not simply what you see: it has powerful links to mood and emotion. Blues and greens – such close reminders of sky and land – bring home a feeling of nature's tranquillity. The jewel-like quality of the turquoise, sapphire, and emerald glass beads that make this lustrous door curtain is intensified by sunlight, so that vivid color is drawn inside while harsh light is filtered to create an impression of coolness and shade. Better still, blue is traditionally said to repel flies.

WHAT YOU NEED

GLASS BEADS

WOODEN BATTEN
1IN (2.5CM) THICK

ELECTRIC DRILL & BIT

COUNTERSINK BIT

STAPLE GUN & STAPLES

STRONG UNWAXED
THREAD

NEEDLE

SCREWDRIVER

BRASS SCREWS

1 Before you start making the curtain, experiment with a variety of beads in different materials, colors, sizes, and shapes to create a design that pleases you (a cloth laid over the work surface will prevent the beads from rolling around). The thread you are using must be unwaxed so that the beads are tightly held. Check to be sure.

2 Measure the inside of the door frame, and cut the wooden batten to fit. To provide fixing points for the bead strings, mark evenly spaced holes along the face of the batten; the distance between them will depend on the size of the beads and the density of curtain you want. Drill and countersink the holes. Use a staple gun to fix a staple firmly across each hole.

3 Cut a length of unwaxed thread twice the desired length of the curtain plus 2in (5cm). Pass the first bead along to the center of the thread. Bring one side of the thread up around the bead to meet the other side and knot the two tightly together close to the bead hole.

4 Thread the resulting double thread through the needle. To make up the first bead string, thread beads according to your design through the needle onto the string, leaving 2in (5cm) at the end. Make more strings, counting the beads on each to make sure it is the correct length.

5 To attach a bead string to the batten, pass one end of its thread through a staple and knot it securely to the other end: the nearest bead should hang just below the batten. Attach the remaining strings to the batten, then screw it, face in, to the inside of the door frame.

Earth tones

THERE IS AN abundance of vivid color in nature, which you can reflect at home, but restful tones of cream, gray, and brown have intrinsic beauty that is timeless and easy to live with. Our pleasure in neutral colors has much to do with an appreciation of natural materials: of ocher and umber earth pigments, and the grays and creams that recall the color and texture of weathered stone.

Natural tones work well together, and there is enough choice in this color palette for you to feel no restriction. Peaceful shades of buff, camel, and biscuit offer simple sophistication. If you want to add strong color, those of a similar earthy quality, such as terra-cotta and jet black, work best. Complement the colors with your choice of materials, selecting naturally earth-toned slate and stone, wood, rush matting, raw silk, and unbleached cotton.

FEMININE ELEGANCE
Right, The flattering glow of soft buff pink natural plaster walls is fitting in a traditionally feminine bedroom. Married with delicately subdued floral prints, checked bedskirt, and sumptous brocade at the windows, the effect is irresistibly elegant rather than sugary.

HANDMADE QUILT
A delicate quilt carries the colors of the room in an exquisite, complex design.

Maintain a visual link with the outside world, for

REFLECTED GREENS
Above left This paneled drawing room in neutral tones is colored by a wash of ethereal green light, reflected and softly filtered through trees in the garden outside.

SEASIDE SIMPLICITY
Above center No sea green or luminous blue finds a way in here. Instead, the clarity of seaside light is celebrated in a room that reflects the soothing hues of driftwood and shells.

STUDIED OBJECTS
Above right In a stylized, highly ordered setting, the rich tones of wood combine with pale walls to illustrate the elegance of the natural palette.

RUSTIC KITCHEN
Left A sweep of deep red brown on uneven plaster walls is a rustic treatment for a humble kitchen. It is very effective with the gentle tones and textures of worn, polished wood and terra-cotta tiles.

a sense of color is learned from the landscape.

Surfaces

Thinking about surfaces

SURFACES AND DECORATIVE details should enrich our homes by delighting the eye, and – since beauty is tactile as well as visual – they should be satisfying to touch. Indeed, it has been said that we need to touch and be touched to ensure our well-being.

Materials from the natural world transform houses into living, breathing spaces. Choose those that are sustainable, especially timber, which must be sourced from managed plantations. For floors and furniture, wall cladding, window-frames, and inner doors, indigenous hardwoods and softwoods reflect their native surroundings and meld naturally with them, and their harvesting poses no threat to the fragile balance of the environment.

Floors, ceilings, and walls need not be treated alike; instead, create spaces for living that are alive with possibilities, tantalizing every sense with their rich variety of textural interest. A balanced room should function *and* delight, but trusting your own judgment and pleasing yourself is the surest way to get it right: if you like something, it will probably go with what you have. Following your instinct means

The cool kindliness of sheets, that soon smooth

mixing, not always matching, reveling in consequent ambiguities and contradictions. Consider rough and smooth, for example, plaster walls troweled and retaining fine ribs, ridges, and flourishes like white mountain frosting on a cake – or concrete floors polished to a mirror finish. Think practicality, too, in both hard and soft furnishings. Glazed tiles, stainless steel, and marble – all readily washed down – share associations of cleanliness and efficiency that make them first-rate for bathrooms and kitchens; cotton bedlinen is fresh and hygienic whatever the weather.

Note the changes in subtle and inexpensive ways that accentuate, or accommodate, the mood of the season. Wide strips of fine linen shade windows and furnishings from summer's piercing sun, and are easily replaced with heavier drapes in winter; sisal mats – balm for hot feet – can be rolled up and set aside in winter when the oriental rugs come out of storage. Finally, cherish the rug with worn patches, the comfortable sagging chair, and the sun-faded fabrics, for the patina of use is the heart of the home and the soul and memory of those who live in it.

away trouble; and the rough male kiss of blankets.

Rupert Brooke

Floorings

PATTERNED LINOLEUM
Rubber, linoleum, and sealed cork are natural, easy-care materials for floors that need frequent mopping. The linoleum in this bathroom has an inlaid pattern to enliven the all-white paneling.

THE FLOOR MAY BE the first thing your feet touch in the morning, and the last at night; and since the soles of the feet contain thousands of nerve endings, what lies under them is surely important – especially if you like to indulge the healthy practice of going barefoot.

Floorings provide insulation, pattern, texture, and color, and can (if you choose) contribute a natural element to man-made interiors. Hard floors, such as stone and tile, are most hygienic, but can be cold in damp climates; wood, rubber, and cork are warmer, and a kinder underfoot surface for children. Woven floorings, such as sisal, happily absorb the to and fro of shod feet, and are ideal in hallways and on stairs. Pure wool carpet, with a hessian or rubber underlay, adds comfort and elegance to areas of lesser use.

WOOD WITH FINE RUG
Right Polished wood has a warm, soothing quality and ages well, while rugs soften the surface, bring in color, and are easily moved around.

NATURAL SLATE
Below left Hard floors of slate, stone, terracotta or ceramic tiles, or polished and sealed concrete are durable and require very little maintenence.

COIR MATTING
Below right For areas of high traffic (particularly from outside to in), use hard-wearing floorings, such as coir, sisal, rush matting, and seagrass.

The first tactile sensation of the new day may be feeling the floor under your feet.

Hooked rag hearth rug

THE RUG has a knobby texture that is a welcome treat for bare feet.

THE ENTREATY TO *waste not, want not* well describes the frugal and practical origins of rag rugs – traditionally made from pieces of old clothing – but takes little account of the faded beauty and comfortable familiarity that natural fabrics, such as cotton, wool, velvet, and silk, acquire after years of use. The simplest rugs and mats are made from plaited strips of wool or cotton rags, coiled and firmly stitched together. Here, a rug hook is used to secure fabric strips to burlap, creating a hard-wearing rug of bold and simple design, strong color, and pleasing texture. Rag rugs can be washed, carefully, in cold water, and hung over a line to dry.

WHAT YOU NEED

BURLAP

MARKER PEN

FIRM-WEAVE FABRIC

RUG HOOK
(FROM CRAFT SHOPS)

MULTIPURPOSE GLUE

WOOD OR PLASTIC
CLOTHES PEGS

GLASS-HEADED PINS

LARGE NEEDLE &
STRONG THREAD

1 A small rug 2ft (60cm) by 3ft (90cm) is quick and simple for a first go at this technique. If you need design inspiration, look at sources such as postcards, paintings, and illustrations from books (Alison Uttley's *Little Grey Rabbit* inspired this design). Collect all the materials together.

3 To start, use one hand to hold a fabric strip at the back of the burlap; use the other hand to hold the rug hook at the front. Push the hook through the burlap from front to back, and catch the fabric strip in the hook. The picture shows the *back* of the burlap.

5 To finish the edges of the rug, fold the 2in (5cm) border (see Step 2) to the back of the rug. Use multipurpose glue to fix it in place, attaching clothes pegs at the edges to hold the layers of fabric firmly until the glue is dry.

2 Cut the burlap to the desired size plus 2in (5cm) all around to neaten the edges. Use the pen to draw the design onto the the burlap, leaving a 2in (5cm) border (see Step 5). Cut the fabric into a heap of strips about 1in (2.5cm) wide and 18in (45cm) long.

4 Pull the hook and the fabric strip through to the front of the burlap, making a loop about 1in (5cm) long. Take the hook out of the loop, and move it along about 1in (2.5cm). Push the hook through to the back, and pull through a second loop. Repeat, to build up the design.

6 To neaten the back of the rug, cut a piece of burlap to size plus 1in (2.5cm) all around. Turn under the hem, and then pin the burlap to the back of the rug. Use the needle and thread to slip-stitch the backing to the rug.

Walls

FLORAL TRIBUTE
Right If you like pattern, wallpaper is a good way to bring it into a room. Here, fresh flowers and a botanical print follow the exuberant theme.

ADDING VARIETY
• Paneling has an architectural quality that brings interest to a featureless room. It insulates walls to keep in heat, and is robust and practical.

• Sliding doors and folding screens are useful movable walls that can help you to change your space.

WRITE ON THE WALL
Right Paint a whole wall, or even a small part of it, with chalkboard paint to bring creativity back into everyday life – and provide a place to write messages and reminders.

BARE BEAUTY
Far right Plaster, brick, and stone can all be left unfinished to reveal the features of a building's past or simply to display their unadorned beauty.

FOR MOST PEOPLE, walls are fundamental to the idea of shelter. The treatment you apply to walls can help you to feel less confined in a small space, and more at ease in a large one. For example, a narrow hall seems wider when the walls are covered with light-reflecting paint; wallpaper with a large overall pattern makes a grand room feel intimate and welcoming.

Regardless of room size, walls are a background for a huge range of materials, textures, colors, and patterns. Painted walls can be polished with beeswax for a gentle, reflective sheen; or choose the delicate, chalky texture of water-based paints to absorb light. Wallpaper distracts the eye from defects, smoothing out awkward angles and contours. And remember: whatever you do to walls, you can do to ceilings, too.

Fundamental to the idea of shelter, walls are a

FULL COVERAGE
Above For a continuous, pleasing look, apply the same treatment to walls and ceiling. Paint stripes to a customized color and design if you cannot find suitable wallpaper.

ROUGH & SMOOTH
Below An interior wall of rough concrete meets smooth slate tiles on the floor. Light is reflected from both surfaces, and softens the effect of the naturally hard materials.

backdrop to the decorative scheme of a room.

Leaf-printed wall

TENDER young briar rose leaves inspired the design of this charming wall print.

A LOVE OF NATURE is embedded in our consciousness, and a wall patterned with leaves is a poignant yet reassuring reminder that nature is never far away, even in the city. Images of nature help to redress the balance between nature and all that is artificial in modern homes. The repeat pattern of this print is made with a foam rubber stamp; use any size or shape of leaf you like. Little paint is needed, so it makes sense to use left-over odds and ends; or buy a small test pot in a special color. The technique works best on a smooth surface. If you like a distressed finish, rub the wall gently with fine sandpaper once the paint is dry.

1 A simple leaf shape is easiest for cutting out and printing. Photocopy the leaf onto thick paper; you can reduce or enlarge the original size as you please. Use a craft knife to cut out the paper leaf shape. Place it on the foam rubber, and draw around the outline.

2 Use multipurpose glue to fix the foam rubber to a piece of hardboard of the same size. Before the foam rubber has stuck to the hardboard, cut around the shape, using the craft knife, through the foam rubber layer only. Cut out any details, such as small teeth at the leaf edges.

3 When the glue is dry, turn over the piece of hardboard and draw a line precisely down its center. Using the line as a position guide, glue a small block of wood to the center back of the hardboard to form a handle, and leave to dry. The printing stamp is now ready for use.

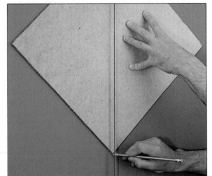

4 To position the design at regular intervals on the wall, cut a square of hardboard to the size of the desired pattern interval. Hang a plumb line at the top of the wall. When it stops swinging, place the square behind it and mark the four corners. Repeat the marks across the wall.

5 Pour the paint into a shallow container. Use a small piece of synthetic sponge to apply a layer of paint to the leaf shape on the printing stamp; try to keep paint away from the hardboard surface.

6 Hold the stamp by its handle and, using the pattern repeat marks as a guide, press the stamp flat to the wall to create the first motif. Hold the stamp firmly against the wall for a few seconds to get a good impression, then remove it in a swift motion. Repeat, to complete the pattern.

Liming wood

IN THE SIXTEENTH and seventeenth centuries, lime or whitewash was applied to wood and plaster to protect the surface – a technique that was revived by the Arts and Crafts movement in the nineteenth century.

Today, it is possible to recreate a limed effect by working liming wax (or white latex paint) deep into the grain of wood, then removing it almost at once. Liming leaves a silvery bloom on floorboards and furniture. It works best on open-grained wood, such as oak, chestnut, and ash, that has not been polished, varnished, or lacquered. Since paint dries fast, work on a small area at a time if you are using it. You can emphasize the grain of limed wood by rubbing the surface with medium-grade steel wool.

◄ STEP 1: OPEN THE GRAIN
Working in the direction of the grain, gently distress the wood with a wire brush so that more wax or paint can be absorbed.

▼ STEP 2: RUB IN LIMING MATERIAL
Use medium-grade steel wool or a stiff bristle brush and a circular motion to apply the wax or paint. Remove any that is not absorbed.

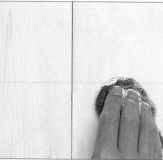

STEP 3: PROTECT & BUFF
If you are using paint, allow to dry. Use a lint-free soft cloth to apply a protective coat of clear wax, then polish with a soft-bristled brush.

LIMING WAX
Prepared liming wax is available from specialist craft shops.

Painted garden table & chairs

ANY SHADE of green, be it peppermint, pea, olive, or lime, is easy on the eye.

WEATHERED WOOD may have a certain visual appeal, but sooner or later outdoor furniture needs some renovation and a lick of paint. These garden chairs are made from wooden slats screwed to a metal frame. Not everything has to match, and a metal table is a good partner for them. It is possible to combine a variety of furniture styles and still create a strong visual statement. When choosing the color of paint, consider the colors around you, and observe how color appears in nature. Green is an obvious choice for garden furniture and very versatile, or look to the sky, sea, or flower borders and beds for abundant inspiration.

WHAT YOU NEED

RUBBER GLOVES
SMALL PAINTBRUSH
PAINT STRIPPER
PAINT SCRAPER
OLD NAILBRUSH
COARSE WIRE WOOL
SYNTHETIC SPONGE
SANDPAPER
EXTERIOR-GRADE
PAINT

1 To prepare the wooden parts for painting, work in a well-ventilated place, preferably outdoors. Wear heavy-duty rubber gloves to protect your hands; if you are sensitive to fumes, wear a dust mask as well. Use a small paintbrush to apply paint stripper to the wooden parts; take care to follow the manufacturer's instructions on the tin.

2 When the stripper has worked, the old paint will look wrinkled; test with the edge of the scraper to see if the paint lifts readily. If not, leave a little longer. To remove the old paint, scrape in the direction of the wood grain. Take care not to dig the edge of the scraper into the wood.

3 Use an old nailbrush with nylon bristles (or a toothbrush) for areas that are particularly hard to reach, such as between the slats. Where the paint is stubbornly ingrained, take a wad of coarse wire wool, dip it in paint stripper, and rub the wood in the direction of the grain.

4 If necessary, strip old paint from the metal parts in the same way. Prepare a bucket of warm soapy water and carefully sponge all parts of the chair to remove any paint stripper that remains on the surface. Rinse with plain water, and then leave the chair to dry thoroughly.

5 If necessary, prepare the surface for painting by lightly sanding rough parts. Brush off any debris, then wipe with a damp sponge; leave to dry. Following the manufacturer's instructions on the tin, apply as many coats of paint as needed, leaving the paint to dry between coats.

Furniture

RUSH-SEATED CHAIR
This charming chair is functional, comfortable, and decorative, too. Old furniture is often more satisfying (and of better quality) than pieces that are mass produced.

WITH FURNITURE, FUNCTION is a main consideration. It should have pleasing, appropriate proportions, and is ideally *multi*functional: tables should be big enough to eat and work at; sofas should be generously sized, inviting you to share them with friends or stretch out on them at the end of the day.

Too often, though, we surround ourselves with an assortment of furniture that reflects neither our taste nor our personality. Think of furniture as you would your clothes. Consider the shape and texture (as well as the comfort) of each piece, and get rid of what you do not like, even if it is still serviceable; it can always be recycled in another home. To bring fresh life into a room, go beyond familiar styles: wicker, rattan, and bamboo furniture introduces a touch of the exotic, is inexpensive, and looks good both inside and out.

Consider the shape and texture as well as the comfort of each piece.

TRADITIONAL STYLE
Left Your own choice of furniture brings interest and character to a room, creating a strong visual statement. This bedroom invites relaxation in the gently curved lines of a padded headboard, bow-fronted chest of drawers, bedside tables, and stool with scroll legs.

KEY WITH TASSEL
A pretty tassel attached to a key turns it into a small ornament for this chest.

DRAMATIC SIMPLICITY
Left The furnishings of
this dining room match
its spaciousness in their
boldness and simplicity.
Real drama comes from
the still-life canvas on the
wall, and an impressive
arrangement of flowers
on the column table.

VARIATIONS ON A THEME
The robust textures of a low
wooden bench, ladder-back
chairs with rush seats, and a
long refectory table establish
a strong theme.

FLOOR & CEILING
Wide polished planks on the
floor echo the color, form,
knots, and grain of the wood
ceiling beams.

DOWN TO BUSINESS
Far left No clutter is to
be seen in this business-
like corner. Its efficiency
is emphasized by clean,
minimal furnishings; a
simple table for a desk
and a low-backed chair
upholstered in smooth
natural-colored linen.

RUSTIC WITH SPIRIT
Left This kitchen has a
cozy feeling that comes
(at least in part) from the
use of natural materials.
The china cabinet and
far wall are painted in
sympathetic rather than
matched color tones.

Visual texture

THERE IS MORE to texture than what you feel when you touch a surface – hard or soft, rough or smooth, cool or warm. Texture also has a visual quality (the interplay of light and dark; the layering of color, tone, and pattern) that brings vitality, interest, and imagination into the decor of your home.

Pattern can, therefore, be called *visual texture*, but choosing and coordinating it is often bewildering, since the possibilities are endless. Harmony is easily achieved if you begin with a single color, or piece of fabric or wallpaper, and add toning patterns and textures. It is difficult to assess the impact of a pattern on a room from small sample squares, so invest in larger pieces and take the time to gather a multitude of swatches before deciding what is right for you.

TONING COLOR
The blue-green paintwork of the washstand picks out one of the wallpaper colors in a toning shade. It is a striking contrast to the pale colors displayed on the wall.

COOL CONTRAST ON THE VERANDA
Abundant pattern decorates every surface of the summerhouse, illustrated in the sequence of pictures at right. In contrast, the veranda is more simply appointed, with wooden paneling on the walls, a checked tablecloth and napkins, and mismatched china.

MIX & MATCH PATTERN
Use a plain pattern with a busy one to soften its effect. Here, the exuberant energy of roses and delphiniums on the curtain fabric is diffused with an understated blue and white, checked cotton lining.

AN EXUBERANCE OF FLOWERS IN A SUMMERHOUSE

This summerhouse lends itself perfectly to an exuberance of floral pattern, creating a gentle, languid mood that is just right for its use. The wallpaper was chosen first, providing the color theme: a palette of soft pinks, greens, blues, and whites. Fabrics were then added, bit by bit, with checks to counteract overblown roses, all in colors that unite the whole to make a delightfully informal living space.

LAYERED PAINTWORK
On the old iron day bed, the patina of layered, worn, and chipped paint is more appealing than the smooth surface of new paintwork. The old paint that shows through harmonizes with the color scheme.

PLAIN FLOORING
The expanse of unadorned polished pine floorboards provides a foil to the many patterns that cover almost every surface of the room, in the wallpaper, bedlinen, throws, soft furnishings, and decorative accessories.

FLORALS & STRIPES
Comfortable cushions piled onto wicker chairs on the veranda, and on the bed, continue the theme of the wallpaper and curtain fabric in their complementary mix of pink, blue, green, and off-white florals and stripes.

Working with pattern

EMBELLISHED DRAWER
Decorating a cupboard with a simple stenciled design is an easy way to introduce pattern into an otherwise plain room.

THE POSSIBILITIES FOR mixing and matching pattern are limited only by your imagination. There are no rules – except to have fun, trust your intuition, and choose patterns that make you feel good. Accents of pattern can be introduced with cushions of different prints, weaves, and colors; then simply add fabrics, wallpaper, or soft furnishings to layer the effect.

To begin with, it is easiest to work with a small palette of two or three colors, or a tonal range of one color. If a dominant pattern or highly colored design is your starting point, support it with simpler motifs or muted tones. Consider scale, but do not be bound by it. A large, bold print in a small room or a tiny overall pattern in a large one can be a refreshing change of pace and an unexpected delight.

TOILE DE JOUY
Right Courageous use of a large pattern in a tiny room breaks the rules to great effect. Here, *toile de Jouy* is used in the typical way, as both fabric and wallpaper, and is further embellished with a frieze and corona of shells.

HAPPY ASSOCIATION
Far right The informality of checks in clear, fresh hues suits simple window treatments, such as this roller blind. Checks go happily with florals, and most other pattern, for a look that is understated and yet quietly elegant.

There are no rules except to trust your intuition

STRONG PERSONALITY
Above The owner of this room has a strong sense of style as well as a firm grasp on what she likes. Stenciled walls, curtains hand-blocked with the same design, and richly textured fabrics make a combination that brooks very little argument.

YOUTHFUL SIMPLICITY
Right The square is the symbol of harmony, and it may be the repetition of this device that gives checks a lasting appeal. Here, a bold blue on the tablecloth is repeated in larger checks painted on the wooden floor.

and choose patterns that make you feel good.

Stenciled sunflower table linen

REPRODUCE the motif in a simpler form: it will have all the charm of the original.

ONCE YOU HAVE mastered the art of stenciling, you can use the technique on any surface or material to transform a room with minimum expense and to maximum effect. Begin with this table cloth or a paper cloth to enliven a party table – the technique is the same – or use your own motif to revitalize a dull armchair, coordinate existing furnishings, or extend a decorative theme. Avoid synthetic and textured fabrics. Cotton is the most suitable for stenciling, washed and ironed before you start. Hand-wash the finished cloth in cool soapy water, or select a delicates cycle if you want to wash it by machine.

WHAT YOU NEED

DRAWING PAPER

STENCIL CARD OR ACETATE

MASKING TAPE

CUTTING MAT

CRAFT KNIFE

DRESSMAKER'S PINS

COTTON FABRIC

STENCIL BRUSHES

FABRIC PAINTS

1 For a stenciled design, each color must have a separate stencil: for this design, three stencils are needed. Draw the design onto paper, and then tape a sheet of acetate or card on top. Mark a solid line to indicate one color; mark dotted lines to indicate the other two colors.

2 Indicate the other two colors on two more sheets of stencil material in the same way. Lay the first stencil sheet on the cutting mat, using tape to secure it. With the craft knife, cut out the part of the design indicated by the solid line. Cut out the other stencil sheets in the same way.

3 Use pins to accurately indicate the position of the motifs on the cloth. Working with the palest color first, tape the stencil sheet to the fabric so that the stencil does not move about. Use a stencil brush to apply the first color of paint: a dabbing action will work it into the fabric.

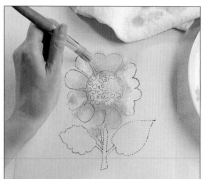

4 Repeat the first color for all the motifs; leave the paint to dry. To apply the next color, tape the second stencil sheet over the motif; take care to align the dotted lines accurately over the outline of the first color. Apply the second color in the same way as the first (see Step 3).

5 Repeat stenciling the second color for all the motifs; leave until dry. Follow the instructions in Step 4 to place the third stencil sheet and apply the final color (for each step, keep a rag handy to wipe excess paint off the brush). When all the motifs have been stenciled, leave the cloth to dry flat overnight.

6 Follow the instructions with the fabric paints to fix the colors so that they will not run when the cloth is washed. The usual method is to iron the cloth on the wrong side, using a dry iron at a specified heat setting. To finish the cloth, fringe the edges or turn and stitch a small hem.

Air

Thinking about air

THE SKY IS THE one visual constant in life for every creature on the planet. We are inclined to think of the atmosphere as without substance, *as light as air*, yet air is composed of million upon million atoms of gases, including the oxygen we breathe.

We are justified in feeling anxious about the air we breathe, given undisputed scientific evidence of atmospheric pollution. For many years, the quality of outside air was of most concern. We now know that synthetic building materials, adhesives, paints, fabrics, furnishings, and all manner of chemicals used in cleaning products pollute the insides of our homes, and combine with emissions from electrical equipment to do us harm.

A constant flow of fresh, clean air through your home will help to prevent the build-up of stale and polluted air. Open doors and windows wide to get air circulating. Use draft-proofing and insulation where necessary to keep the house snug and warm, but never stop up air vents: buildings must breathe, too. Efficient ventilation is particularly important in kitchens and bathrooms, replacing moist air, which

Clear the air! clean the sky! wash the wind!

encourages bacteria and mold, with cool clean air to keep the room fresh and dry. Essential oils, such as tea tree and lavender, have natural antibacterial and disinfectant properties. They are ideal to diffuse in moist environments, and a pleasant alternative to chemical cleansers and sprays. Many cultures prize essential oils for their gently therapeutic effects and ability to revitalize or soothe both mind and body. Houseplants also improve the quality of inside air. They release oxygen, absorb the carbon dioxide we breathe out, and are natural humidifiers.

Domestic chores are part of cherishing the private world of home, so they should be enjoyable as well as part of household routine. Try to avoid chemical cleansers, considering natural ones instead. Vinegar and water makes windows sparkle; baking soda has a hundred uses, from refreshing a stale refrigerator to scouring a grimy bathtub until it gleams. Use natural products for their delicious, lingering scent when the cleaning is done, buffing floors and furniture with homemade rosemary beeswax polish, handwashing delicate linens with your own clove and honey soap.

Take stone from stone and wash them ...

Thomas Stearns Eliot

Circulation

HEALTHY PLEASURE
To enjoy the fragrant summer garden through doors flung wide is not simply a pleasure: it also helps to make the house a healthier place.

TO BE HEALTHY, a house must be allowed to breathe. Increasing the movement of air within it can help to make you more healthy, too. With energy-efficient strategies, air conditioning, and nonporous building materials, pollutants and stale air quickly build up in the home, so that the constant circulation of clean, fresh air becomes a vital necessity.

Make the best use of interior and exterior doors, windows, and vents so that fresh air is drawn into the house and stale air can escape. Open windows wide whenever the weather permits. Keep the air moving to prevent stuffiness, but beware of drafts. Still air promotes the growth of mold and bacteria. You can discourage them by diffusing lavender or tea tree oil (both are antibacterial) in burners or candles.

CASEMENT & SASH WINDOWS
Windows let in air and light, shut out drafts and cold, and are an important feature in every room. Insulating windows, for example with double glazing, prevents heat from escaping during the cold months, and keeps a house cool when it is hot outside. These drawings illustrate the two main types of windows.

MAXIMIZE WHAT YOU HAVE
If you have sash windows, open them so that fresh air can enter at the bottom, while hot, stale air can escape at the top.

AIR CONDITIONING
• Electric fans are an energy-efficient way to cool a room. Old-fashioned table and ceiling fans are elegant, too.

• If your home is air-conditioned, put bowls of water here and there. A healthy environment needs some moisture.

• Central heating dries the air. Set the temperature lower, and supplement it with heat from an open fire or stove.

Draw fresh air

AIRY COMFORT
Above Venetian blinds in this bathroom allow the door and window to be open to admit fresh air, while steam escapes and the bather's privacy and comfort are maintained.

STRATEGIC PLANNING
Right With heat from the stove and cooking smells, a kitchen should be very well aired and ventilated (open windows wide for a short while every day). The strategically placed windows in this kitchen provide a free passage of air throughout the room.

SAFE COOKING
Ensure a constant exchange of air in your kitchen if you are cooking with gas.

AT THE READY
Use the heat from the stove to dry and air towels and kitchen linens.

CASEMENT WINDOW
An inward- or outward-opening casement window gives maximum ventilation because its whole area can be open to the air.

SASH WINDOW
A sash window consists of two vertically sliding panels. Ventilation is reduced because only half the area can be open to the air.

GAUZY NIGHTS
Far left In a hot climate, sheer, lightweight fabrics shield a four-poster bed but let cool night air flow freely around it through the open balcony door.

CONVERSATION PIECE
Left A soft breeze wafts gently in at an open sash window, draped with the filmiest muslin, providing a pleasant corner to enjoy fresh air or sit and chat.

into the house, and let stale, polluted air escape.

Stamped muslin window panel

THE SUBTLE motif is most effective when natural light streams through the panel.

A GENTLE BREEZE playing at an open bathroom window is lovely on a warm morning. This decorative window panel, made from a scrap of unbleached muslin printed with a simple motif, allows fresh air to enter while diffusing light and retaining your privacy. The inspiration came from an eighteenth-century French wood printing block, but any device can be adapted: cherries, perhaps, or print squares or polka dots. To make your own stamp, follow the instructions in *Leaf-printed wall* (see page 114); or buy a ready made stamp. The panel sides are finished with a looped edging, called picot, and it is hung by curtain wire, hooks, and eyes.

WHAT YOU NEED

UNBLEACHED MUSLIN
DRESSMAKER'S PINS
NEEDLE & THREAD
THIN CARD
LARGE BOARD OR
SHEET OF PAPER
FABRIC PAINT
SYNTHETIC SPONGE
PRINTING STAMP OF
YOUR CHOICE

1 Measure the window recess, and cut a piece of muslin to the required size. Allow extra for a small double hem at the bottom and sides of the panel and a deeper hem at the top: this will form the channel for the curtain wire. Turn a double hem to the wrong side at bottom and sides, pin, tack, and secure with running stitches. Make the hem deeper at the top.

2 To position the motifs on the fabric, cut the card into a square the size of the pattern repeat: if it is 6in (15cm), for example, cut a square of that size. Position the square on the fabric, as shown, and use pins to mark the corners. Move the square over the fabric to mark the position of all the motifs.

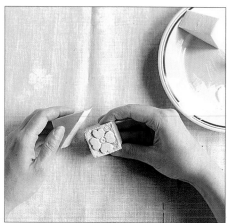

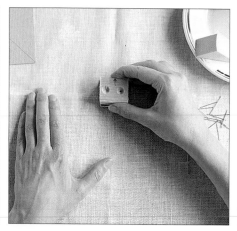

3 Place a board or large sheet of clean paper on the work surface so that paint will not mark the surface. Lay the fabric panel, right side up, on top of the board or paper. Pour the paint into a shallow container. Use a piece of sponge to apply paint sparingly to the printing stamp.

4 Use one hand to keep the fabric in position. For the first motif, press the stamp onto the fabric, hold for a few seconds, then remove in a swift motion. Repeat for all the motifs until the design is complete. Leave to dry, then fix the paint following the manufacturer's instructions.

5 To make the trim, oversew the edge with three stitches. Insert the needle again, and wind the thread around it seventeen times. Pull the needle through, draw the thread into a tight loop, and fix with a stitch. Make more loops in the same way, spacing three stitches apart.

Memory, scent, & aroma

THERE IS NOTHING more memorable than scents and smells. Often fleeting, scent conjures memories that may bring recollections of childhood to the present, or effectively take us out of time. Scents make gentle reference to intimate history, and with them we can personalize space and make it our own.

We may close our eyes and block our ears, but as long as we breathe, we can smell. The effect of smell is immediate, and (as with the other senses) perhaps the fastest way to our emotions, since it is undiluted by body language and words. Who would attempt to describe all the nuances of smell? In your home, go for natural rather than artificial or "nature-identical" smells, and use fragrant essential oils extracted from plants to revitalize body and mind, and scent the air.

FRESH-BAKED BREAD
Smell and taste are close relatives: if you lose your sense of smell, you forfeit much of the pleasure in food. Fresh-baked bread has a smell that is known for its feel-good effect.

HERBAL ESSENCES
Left Green scents, from flowers, fragrant herbs, and scented plants, are naturally uplifting. Use potted herbs and plants in the kitchen to revive you while you work.

FIRESIDE MEMORY
Right Dried citrus peels make good lighters for a wood fire. When the fire is ablaze, their spiciness mingles with the warm fragrance of the wood.

FRAGRANT LINEN
Far right Newly washed and ironed clothes smell wonderfully fresh. Avoid softeners, and tuck sprigs of rosemary or lavender among towels and linen to prolong the scent.

Scents make gentle reference to our intimate past,

HERBS TO STIMULATE
Left Sage, thyme, cedar wood, rosemary, juniper, and eucalyptus enhance vitality and aid stamina. Bergamot and neroli are motivating and uplifting.

HERBS TO BALANCE
Right Peppermint can be used alone, or combined with orange or lavender to help restore a sense of perspective.

VAPORIZING OILS
Left Use essential oils in a special vaporizer or light bulb ring, or add to bath water to make a veil of heady scented steam.

HERBS TO SOOTHE
Right Orange, marjoram, cardamom, sandalwood, vetiver, patchouli, myrrh, and frankincense soothe and comfort. Blend them together as you wish.

and are an appealing way to personalize a room.

Rosemary beeswax polish

THIS NATURAL HERBAL preparation is an effective alternative to commercial polishes, which often contain an unpleasant mix of synthetic and chemical ingredients. Rosemary was cultivated in ancient Greek and Roman gardens as much for its antibacterial, purifying properties as for its pungent, aromatic, resinous scent, which is said to intoxicate bees. To make the polish, an infusion of rosemary is combined with pure turpentine, beeswax, and soapflakes, so that the polish acts as a cleanser, too. Use a soft cloth to apply it sparingly to wood, metal, or painted surfaces, then buff to a deep, lasting shine with a clean, soft cloth.

CHOOSE a sunny spot to grow rosemary, in memory of its Mediterranean origin.

WHAT YOU NEED

10FL OZ (300ML) PURE TURPENTINE

HEAT RESISTANT BOWL

SAUCEPAN

2OZ (60G) BEESWAX

LARGE HANDFUL OF FRESH ROSEMARY

HEAT RESISTANT JUG

2OZ (60G) SOAPFLAKES

TWO 1LB (500G) SCREW-TOP GLASS JARS

1 Pour the turpentine into the bowl. Pour a small amount of very hot water into the saucepan, and set the bowl over it: the bowl should not touch the water. Use a board and a large kitchen knife to cut the beeswax into chunks.

2 Add the beeswax to the turpentine in the bowl. Place the saucepan over a gentle heat so that the water just simmers: it must not boil. Leave until the beeswax has melted (there is no need to stir), then set aside to cool.

3 To make the rosemary infusion, place the herb (with stalks) into the jug. Bring 8fl oz (250ml) water to the boil, then pour the boiling water over the rosemary in the jug. Leave to steep for ten to fifteen minutes, pressing the rosemary down into the water, if necessary.

4 Place a sieve over a bowl, pour the infusion into it, and press the rosemary with a metal spoon to extract all the liquid. Measure it in a jug; there should be 7fl oz (200ml). Return the warm liquid to the heat resistant jug, add the soapflakes, and stir until dissolved. Leave to cool.

5 Add the cooled rosemary infusion to the mixture of beeswax and turpentine in the bowl. Use a large metal spoon to combine all the ingredients. Pour the mixture into the two jars, and screw on the lids. When thoroughly cold, the polish will have a creamy texture.

Plants & flowers

IN OUR BUSY LIVES, moments to enjoy the benefit and beauty of nature are all too rare. Plants and flowers remind us how fragile life is – how much it deserves nurture and care. Tending and arranging them is an opportunity for contemplation, a time to admire a plant in bloom, or to let flowers lift your spirits with their scent or color. Houseplants refresh the air by replacing carbon dioxide with oxygen; they can help to humidify dry atmospheres and absorb pollutants from cleaning materials. Large-leaved kinds, such as the aroids at right, are the most effective.

◄ PLANTS FOR BRIGHT LIGHT
Begonias (see left), dwarf azaleas, chrysanthemums, gerbera daisies, and tulips are especially useful for providing colorful displays year-round, as well as adding oxygen and moisture to the air. Be careful not to scorch the leaves during the hot summer months.

PLANTS FOR LOW LIGHT ►
Chinese evergreens (see right) and rubber plants are tolerant of low light conditions, and extra care will help them look their best.

LONGER LIFE
Cut flowers will last longer if you change the water frequently.

◄ FRESH FLOWERS
An exuberant arrangement of fresh flowers, leaves, twigs, and berries in season brings the vitality of nature inside to enliven your surroundings.

Aromatic herb & spice wreath

DRY leftover material and put it in drawstring bags to scent closets and drawers.

MAKE GOOD USE of summer's sun to grow herbs in abundance, then harvest them in Fall before the first frosts, and fashion them into this delightful wreath. Create a wreath to scent and decorate your kitchen, or to present to a friend. When dry, the herbs will bring welcome flavour to winter soups and stews. The wreath uses a combination of fresh sage, bay, rosemary, oregano, dried fennel seedheads, dried habañero chillies, star anise, and licorice and cinnamon sticks. Roadside stands and farmer's markets are good places to look for fresh herbs if you cannot grow your own, but remember that herbs do very well in containers outside.

1 Collect all the materials together. Pruning shears are handy to cut woody stems, but you can just use strong scissors. Use the wire cutters to cut short lengths of spool wire to tie up bunches of the herbs (Step 4). Make a hanging loop from string, and knot to the wire wreath frame.

3 To cover the wreath frame, first cut a long piece of string, and knot one end to the outer ring of the frame (or use spool wire). Take a large handful of moss, and roll it into a firm sausage shape. Place it on the frame, then firmly bind the moss with string (or wire) to secure it.

5 To attach the bunches of herbs to the frame, hold one bunch against the inner edge. Use your other hand to push a florist's pin through the stems of the bunch and into the moss. Place the next bunch with the leaves overlapping the stems of the first, and pin as before. Repeat, working in the same direction.

2 Lay each kind of herb in a separate pile. Pick over the herbs, remove any damaged parts, and cut the stems to a uniform length. Place delicate leaves, such as sage, in a small amount of water to prevent them from wilting. Leave all the herbs in separate piles of each kind until Step 4.

4 Repeat until the frame is completely covered; knot the end of the string (or wire) to the frame to finish off. Make up mixed bunches of the herbs, with five to seven sprigs in each one; use the wire to bind the stems of each bunch together. Trim the ends of the stems level to neaten.

6 When the inner edge is completely covered, secure bunches of herbs to the outer edge in the same way. When the outer edge is covered, attach the dried herbs and spices to the frame. Use florist's pins for the chillies, seedheads, and star anise; sticks of licorice and cinnamon can be pushed in here and there.

Humidity

MOVE THE AIR
Hot air rises. A powerful ceiling fan is at the right height to disperse hot or stale air, and prevents it from building up while circulating fresh air.

THIS SOMETIMES SEASONAL condition has to do with the level of moisture in the air. With high humidity, the air is saturated with moisture and feels wet; with low humidity, the air is uncomfortably dry because it lacks moisture. You may encounter both conditions, depending on climate and how you heat your home.

Low humidity (the core problem of "sick building syndrome") is generally caused by central heating, and can lead to respiratory ailments. Turn down the heating, and increase moisture levels with bowls of water, vaporizers, and houseplants, which are natural humidifiers. High humidity encourages the fungi and molds that are a major cause of allergy in sensitive people, and can damage buildings. Let fresh, cool air circulate through your home, and allow it to breathe by draft-proofing rather than sealing it.

Low humidity

TROPICAL LIVING
Right This comfortably proportioned dining and living space has all that is necessary to improve air quality. All the windows open wide to let in fresh air, two ceiling fans keep it moving, and abundant plants replenish oxygen in the atmosphere.

AVOIDING ROT
Tropical hardwoods, such as iroko and rubber wood, are especially suitable in a bathroom since they have natural water-repellent and antibacterial properties.

NEAT VENT
Right The small internal window in this bathroom is strategically placed at the side of the tub, and can pivot to allow steam to escape and fresh air to enter. A circular skylight sheds light and opens to prevent stuffiness.

KEEP IT FRESH
Improve air quality in your home by opening windows morning and evening.

CHECK & BALANCE

- Some moisture in the air is necessary for a healthy home. A hygrometer checks humidity levels, and can be inexpensively purchased from a hardware shop.

- Consider using a humidifier if your indoor atmosphere is too dry.

- If damp is a real problem, look to the cause instead of just treating the effects.

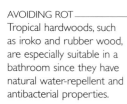

NATURAL EXCHANGE
Left A fire is a reassuring and welcoming symbol of home, but it is much more than just a means of ensuring heat. While the fire both warms and dries surrounding air, its chimney draws fresh air and oxygen into a room and provides an escape for carbon dioxide.

GENEROUS FLUE
Left A stove of almost commercial proportions is a must for the serious cook, and anyone who loves entertaining. Make sure the flue is generous enough to cope with the demand for ventilation and, if necessary, install a ducted hood as well.

MOISTURE CONTROL
Underfloor heating will not dry the air, and does away with cold.

can be the cause of tiresome respiratory ailments.

Moisture

EVEN IF THE other rooms in your house are warm, airy, and dry, the bathroom is a place where you are almost sure to find moisture. This is a room that needs careful planning, and deserves special consideration if it is to be a pleasant, wholesome environment for people and furnishings alike.

The spacious room shown here is an example of such care. Framed drawings on the walls, as well as the books and photographs, might more commonly be enjoyed in a drier atmosphere, yet here there is a good cross-current of ventilation from the window and door, and heat from a sensibly sized radiator and towel rail, to combat steam and condensation. The chair is a moisture-proof combination of chrome and canvas, and all the surfaces are easily mopped.

ENCLOSED LIGHTING
Electrical fixtures and moisture are not a happy mix, so safety in the bathroom is paramount. These opaque glass globes fully enclose the light bulbs: there is no danger of water getting in.

DEDICATED SHOWER COMPARTMENT
In the bathroom pictured at right, the wall opposite the window is dedicated to a large shower compartment; a toilet stands nearby. The step-in shower has no door but a deep sill to contain water, and falls short of the ceiling so that rising steam can escape.

TIGHT-FITTING CUPBOARDS
The doors of the low-level built-in cupboards are fitted with magnetic catches for a tight fit. The cupboards keep a stack of clean towels, toilet paper, and other necessities dry and on hand.

CLIMATE CONTROL IN A BATHROOM

The very colors of this bathroom suggest an airy quality, which is underpinned by a range of practical solutions to moisture. Walls and paneling have a matte finish that discourages condensation; chrome and glass fixtures are safe against moist air; lights are enclosed; and the shower (below left) is kept separate.

OPEN WINDOWS
High humidity and still air encourage bacterial growth and mold. Have windows open whenever possible to exchange fresh dry air for moisture-laden steam. Pull down a blind for privacy.

BENEFICIAL PLANTS
Houseplants refresh the air, and there are many kinds that enjoy the high humidity of a bathroom. Wax-leafed stephanotis (above) is moisture loving – and exquisitely fragrant. To one side of the bath (left), a huge yucca is clearly flourishing.

SENSIBLE FURNISHINGS
This chair has a chrome frame; the seat, back, and arms are upholstered in thick canvas with a close weave. Choose bathroom fabrics and materials with care: many deteriorate or rot in the moist, damp air.

CANDLE VAPORIZER
Lavender and tea tree oils have antibacterial qualities as well as a delicious scent. A candle vaporizer is a safe way to enjoy their healing benefits in a bathroom.

HEATED TOWEL RAIL
Never leave damp and wet towels in a heap: allow them to dry out before the next use. A heated towel rail will dry, air, and warm them, and provides gentle background heat for the room.

Household clove & honey soap

PRESENT the finished soap as a gift, wrapped in waxed paper or tied with raffia.

A COLD OR RAINY DAY, when there is little to enjoy outside, is a good time to linger near a warm stove, in a kitchen fragrant with the mixing and molding of this aromatic soap. Cloves are the dried, unopened flower buds of an evergreen myrtle. Both flower buds and leaves are distilled to make oil of cloves. Antiseptic and pungent, it combines with honey and soapflakes to make a gentle soap that lathers well, and is every bit as good for soothing the work-worn hands of gardeners as it is for hand-washing delicate fabrics. If you prefer their scent to that of cloves, lavender and rosemary have similarly antiseptic properties.

1 If you do not generally use soapflakes, buy the type that are intended for hand-washing clothes: do not use any other kind of washing soap or detergent. The honey need not be a special variety: a blended one is fine. Measure out the soapflakes, and place them in a dish.

3 Pour the water out of the saucepan; wipe it dry. Transfer the mixture to the saucepan, and continue to heat the mixture gently until a stiffish paste forms. Use the wooden spoon to stir and turn the mixture so that it does not catch fire and burn onto the bottom of the saucepan.

5 Rub the insides of the tartlet pans with a bit of corn oil to prevent the dough from sticking. Divide the dough in half, and press one half into a pan, firming it well in to the sides with your thumbs. Rub a drop or two of corn oil over the surface to smooth it. Shape and smooth the other half.

2 Put the soapflakes into the bowl, and measure in the corn oil and honey. Put the bowl over (but not touching) some simmering water in the saucepan, and set over a gentle heat. Stir with a wooden spoon until a soft mass forms, about fifteen minutes. Add the oil of cloves to the mixture.

4 Turn the mixture out onto a wooden board or work surface, and leave to cool slightly. When the mixture is cool enough to handle, use your hands to press and knead it into a smooth, firm "dough."

6 Press a wooden stamp firmly into the surface of the dough to decorate; this is fun to do, especially if the soap is a gift, but not essential. Turn the cakes of soap out of the pans, then leave in a warm, dry place for a week or two before use. Store between towels or linen to retain the scent.

Sound

Thinking about sound

WE LIVE IN A LANDSCAPE of familiar and reassuring sound, for few things on earth are silent. We enjoy foods that crunch, and clink glasses in celebration. When a cat purrs, we feel content, too. Sound has a powerful effect. The rhythmic crash of ocean waves reinforces our connection with nature; the moaning of a fog horn in the sound strikes an eerie note of unease. A mother's heartbeat and the rush of blood lull the baby in her womb. And we form sound into words so that we can communicate ideas, thoughts, and feelings with our fellow human beings.

Sound, then, is part of the sensory stew of our lives, and we depend on it to experience the world outside our own front door. Exposure to unpleasant sound (which we can call *noise*) leads sometimes to illness, and some people seek permanent sanctuary from the bustle of life in the big city, where the endless strain of blocking out noise takes its toll.

Too little sound from outside can lead to feelings of unease and isolation, but you still want to ensure quiet in your home. Solid exterior walls (which help to shield you from the raised voices of quarrelsome

I shall always remember those quiet nights.

neighbors and the throb of heavy traffic) are often not a feature of modern housing. Carpets, rugs, and soft furnishings are an effective and decorative way to provide extra insulation, and also help to save on fuel costs; wood paneling soundproofs ceilings and walls. Remember that hard floorings can cause echo and hard-edged sound, and rarely forgive a dropped plate. If you delight in their beauty and practicality, soften them with layers of rugs. Heavy curtains are an easy way to limit noise, but take care to balance your need for light and air with screening sound.

Pleasant sound will always be culturally defined, yet all sound begins with movement. The gentle to and fro of a wind chime, hung wherever it will catch the breeze, is as soothing as the resonance of its music. For most of us, music is an important part of living well. Lucky people make their own, but we can all have the band or orchestra in our home, thanks to technology. An ancient Chinese proverb says: *a bird does not sing because it has an answer. It sings because it has a song.* The sound of laughter is your own song. Fill your home with it to feel your spirits soar.

To us, the essence of comfort was quietness.

Laura Ashley

Noise & echo

CONSTANT NOISE CONVEYS the hustle and bustle of the modern world into every part of a house – and while *noise* is an unpleasant aspect of life, it would be strange to live in a world without *sound*. Even in a city home, you can find ways to shut out intrusive noise and create your own haven of peace and calm.

Insulation is an obvious starting point. It helps to exclude external noise, and also absorbs echo, which is the uncomfortable sound equivalent of glare from light. Felt or rubber underlays provide insulation and prolong the life of carpets; rugs soften the sound of footsteps on hard floors. Soft furnishings are barriers to noise, as are walls lined with pictures or books. Try using similar strategies in large rooms and open-plan spaces, which have a natural tendency to echo.

DOUBLE BLINDS
Slatted wooden blinds and fabric roman blinds combine to muffle the roar of traffic below. To regulate light and air, they can be used either singly or together.

SOFT FURNISHINGS
Pillows and sofa throws in soft, cushiony fabrics, such as velvet, wool, mohair, chenille, and cashmere, absorb sound. Here, their rich color adds a touch of opulence to the otherwise restrained interior.

COMPACT KITCHEN WITH SUSPENDED UNITS
The kitchen area of the flat pictured at right lies behind the table, opposite the fireplace. It is lined with copious cupboards both above and below eye level. Filled with essential food, crockery, pots, pans, and cleaning materials, they also help to absorb unwanted sound.

RESTFUL CITY APARTMENT

This one-room apartment is above a busy street, but you might never know it. In insulating the windows, floor, and inner walls, every possible consideration has been given to the need for peace and quiet both here and in the apartment below.

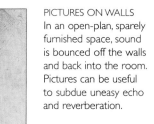

PICTURES ON WALLS
In an open-plan, sparely furnished space, sound is bounced off the walls and back into the room. Pictures can be useful to subdue uneasy echo and reverberation.

BOOK-LINED WALLS
A shelf behind the sofa is crowded with books. Their sound-absorbing quality is continued in wall-to-wall books that line shelves in an area set aside for work.

QUIET FURNITURE
The practical folding chairs are a simple construction of wood slats screwed onto a metal frame. At the ends of the legs, rubber stops form resilient, cushioned feet to prevent noisy scraping and scratching across the hard wood floor.

FLOORBOARDS WITH RUG
Polished floorboards float above the structural floor. Insulation between the two is an effective barrier to the transference of noise from footsteps to the apartment below. Scatter rugs help, too.

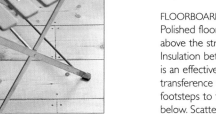

Muffling noise

RESTFUL SLUMBER
Bedrooms should be as quiet as possible: restful, undisturbed sleep is vital for emotional well-being and physical health. This tiny bedroom under the eaves has wood cladding on the walls and ceiling to ensure peace.

GIVEN SOME SAY in the matter, few people would choose to live beside a railway line, next to a power station, or directly under the flight path into an interational airport. When choosing a new house, be aware of these hazards to a quiet home, and of the site: a windy hilltop house is bound to be noisier than one tucked into a valley.

If you have to suffer noisy neighbors or a constant roar of traffic, sound-proofing can dramatically improve the quality of your life. Deal with small annoyances, too. Oil squeaky hinges, fix dripping taps, and bleed central heating radiators if air in the system makes them knock. White sound masks unavoidable noise, and can be useful if noise stops you sleeping. Electronic alarm clocks often have a facility to generate this comforting rush of sound, which is thought to remind us of our time in the womb.

> ### KEEP NOISE OUT
> - Traffic noise is halved with double glazing. A cheaper, less effective, option is secondary glazing.
> - Draft-proof badly fitting windows and doors to reduce both noise and fuel bills.
> - If common walls are not solid, add an extra internal layer.

ARTIST'S COLLECTION
Right Proof against echo, a solid oak bookcase fills the entire wall beside an open stairway. Stacks of books and propped and hung pictures provide an extra layer of insulation.

DIVIDING CURTAIN
Left A thick curtain hung across a room is a simple way to screen off a quiet space and limit noise. In this cottage sitting room, sound is given a soft edge with lustrous woven sisal flooring and plump sofas.

WALL-TO-WALL CARDS
Right Framed postcards cover the walls of a room and the hallway beyond. A thick wooden door is hung on heavy hinges so that it closes quietly, and stops noise from traveling where it is not wanted.

PANELING & TILES
Far right A family kitchen combines insulation with practicality: pine tongue and groove paneling on the walls and ceiling and ceramic tiles on the floor.

Hard floors have appeal, but can be unforgiving.

Hanging a decorative textile

HANDMADE fabrics have a timeless quality that works for any style of interior.

PRECIOUS TEXTILES, RUGS, and cloths often languish forgotten in closets and drawers. Resurrect these irresistible bargains of the weekend flea market and exotic bazaar, and hang them from wooden poles for everyone to enjoy. Wall hangings do more for a room than make a decorative focal point. Even a fragile piece of fabric will help to muffle unwanted, intrusive noise and insulate against drafts if you sandwich a thick layer of cotton batting between it and a heavier lining. Rugs make particularly effective sound absorbers. Recycle an old kilim that is too worn to use; stitch a linen channel to the back to receive the pole.

WHAT YOU NEED

DECORATIVE TEXTILE

LINING FABRIC

1/2IN (12MM) DOWEL ROD

DRESSMAKER'S PINS

NEEDLE & THREADS

TWO DOUBLE-ENDED SCREWS

TWO POPPY SEEDHEADS

TWO CUP HOOKS OR NAILS

1 Ideally, choose a heavy textile, since it will hang better, or line a lightweight piece instead. This hanging is made from two different textiles that complement one another, so that either side can be on view. Treat delicate fabrics gently, and sew them by hand rather than by machine.

2 Make a channel for the rod along the top edge of the textile with lining fabric. Cut the fabric the same width as the textile and deep enough to accommodate the rod, allowing extra for turnings. Turn a small hem to the wrong side along the edges, and press flat.

3 Neatly hand-sew the two short edges, using small running stitches. Lay the textile right side down, top up, on a work surface. Position the fabric channel with its wrong side down, ⅜in (10mm) below the top edge of the textile. Pin, and then tack the long edges.

4 Use a double length of color-matched thread to attach the fabric channel to the textile. If displaying both sides of the texile, use herringbone stitch; pick up only a few threads of fabric each time for a join that is neat and secure. At the ends, fasten off with a knot. Cut the thread close.

5 Slot the dowel rod carefully into the fabric channel, using one hand to push in the rod, and the other to guide the fabric along it. Once the rod is slotted all the way through, it must protrude slightly at either end: this allows it to rest on cup hooks or nails. If the rod is too long, saw a little off the ends.

6 For the finials, screw one end of a double-ended screw into a poppy seedhead, then screw the other end into the rod. Make and attach another finial to the other end of the rod in the same way. To hang the textile, fix cup hooks or nails to the wall, and rest the rod on them.

Natural floorcoverings

FLOORCOVERINGS made from woven plant fibers hark back to medieval times, when floors were strewn with rushes and fragrant herbs. Sisal, hemp, coir, seagrass, and jute carpet and rugs are very hygienic and easily cleaned with a stiff broom. Their natural earth tones and decorative textures complement informal areas of the home, such as this seaside sitting room, where they will gently stimulate bare feet. Use a rubber underlay to increase their life and soundproofing effect.

TO PREPARE A ROUGH SURFACE
You may need to lay hardboard if the existing floor surface is rough.

STEP 1: PREPARE & FIT ▶
Brush water over the sheets of hardboard and leave them for 48 hours where they will be laid. Lay whole sheets first, and then do the edge. Butt a sheet, rough side up, to the skirting board. Mark where the sheet meets those already laid.

◀ STEP 2: CUT SHEETS FOR EDGE
Use a straight edge or steel rule to join the marks on the sheet into a straight line. Then use a steel rule and a heavy craft knife to score the sheet deeply, being careful to follow the line closely. Bend the sheet away from the scoring so that the sheet breaks cleanly. Cut through the backing, if necessary.

STEP 3: STAPLE IN POSITION ▶
Lay the cut sheet smooth side up, and use a staple gun to fix it in position. Cut and fix more sheets in the same way to complete the perimeter edge.

◀ TAKE YOUR CHOICE
Pictured from far left are sisal, coir, jute, and seagrass. All work well in high traffic areas. Narrow lengths with bound edges also make good stair and hall runners.

Pleasant sound

ELECTRIC APPLIANCES
When choosing domestic
appliances or machinery,
make quietness a priority.
A gadget that generates
excessive noise may not
be worth either the time
or the effort it saves.

SOME SOUNDS WE enjoy, others drive us crazy, and no
two people feel the same. Too often we fill our homes
with ugly sounds rather than those that make us feel
comfortable and happy. Gadgets that we have come
to consider a necessity may take ages to put together,
take apart, and clean, and can be terribly noisy: some
food processors reach a level of noise equal to that of
a chain saw heard at close quarters.

There are many ways to introduce pleasant sound
into your home. The delicate sound and movement
of wind chimes and mobiles helps to energize your
surroundings. If you have a garden, plant trees and
shrubs to hear the gentle rustle of leaves in the wind.
Relish the soft babble of an indoor fountain as the
essence of life. Have rooms filled with music. Hide
electric equipment, and enjoy the sound of silence.

SHAKER BROOM
Left Hard floors can be
swept with a well-made
broom – a pleasant and
therapeutic change from
using a vacuum cleaner.
This traditional Shaker
broom hung on the wall
combines function and
order with decoration.

Clap hands to

NONINTRUSIVE PHONE
Right A telephone that
trills rather than shrills,
a kettle that sings when
it comes to a boil, and a
wind-up alarm clock all
produce pleasant sound
rather than irritating or
intrusive noise. Whenever
possible, try to use non-
electrical equipment.

HIDE AWAY NOISE
Left Washing machines, dryers, and dishwashers generate noise for hours at a time. Conceal them in an insulated cupboard, or isolate them wherever they will not be heard. Shut the door behind a gurgling toilet.

TICK-TOCK HOUSE
Below left In the hustle, bustle, and hectic pace of everyday life, we set aside quietness and fill empty spaces with noise. Relish the reassuring, rhythmic ticking of a clock or the singing of birds instead.

RELEASE THE STRAIN
Below Consider leaving the food processor in the cupboard, and releasing the strains of the day by pounding herbs or spices in a mortar, or enjoying the sensuous exercise of kneading bread.

dissipate and clear the air of negative vibrations.

Copper-pipe wind chime

STRINGS of gaily patterned fabric birds, hung with little bells, inspired this design.

MUSIC CHASES AWAY SADNESS and helps to brighten the day. If the sounds of nature feature little in your daily life, you can still make a wind chime to hang from the branch of a tree, beside a doorway, or within the house, where the occasional touch elicits a gentle resonance. It is said that wind chimes create protective and healing energy, even when silent. Look to nature for your materials, choosing the soothing greens and browns that work so well whatever the setting: traditional or modern, rustic or smart. If your wind chime hangs outdoors, the copper will weather and acquire the attractive blue-green patina known as verdigris.

WHAT YOU NEED

COPPER PIPE

PIPE CUTTER OR
SMALL HACKSAW

ELECTRIC OR HAND
DRILL & BIT

PLIERS WITH CUTTING
BLADES

GALVANIZED WIRE

FLAT GLASS BEADS

LEATHER THONG
OR TWINE

1 This wind chime is easy to make; the only tricky bits are cutting the copper pipe and drilling the holes. If you want to create your own design, sketch it first on a sheet of paper. As the work progresses, note any modifications to the design on your original sketch so that it becomes a template for future models.

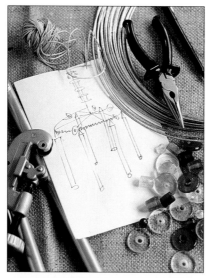

2 Use the pipe cutter or hacksaw to cut seven lengths of copper pipe. If the lengths are all slightly different, as here, the wind chime will produce several tones (longer pipes sound deeper). Use the drill, fitted with an ordinary bit, to drill two small holes opposite each other at both ends of the longest length of pipe. For the other six lengths, drill two holes at one end only. Choose a low-speed setting for an electric drill.

3 With the pliers, cut a length of galvanized wire twice as long as the desired circumference of the finished ring, plus extra to allow for overlapping. Thread six pairs of flat glass beads along the wire, then bend the wire to form a ring, and thread one end back through the beads so that a double thickness of wire runs through them. Knot a piece of the leather thong over the joint, then bind between the first two sets of beads, using blanket stitch as in the picture.

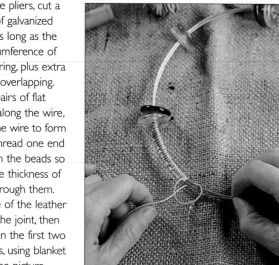

4 Thread a short piece of the leather thong through the two holes in one pipe, and tie in a knot. Attach the pipe to the ring between two of the beads. Continue wrapping leather thong around the ring, attaching five more pipes between beads at even intervals. Thread beads onto a piece of thong, and tie it to one end of the longest pipe; attach a long piece of thong to the other end. Tie six lengths of thong to the ring, and knot together with the central pipe for hanging.

Home comforts

Thinking about comfort

TO MAKE YOUR HOME a comfortable place, you will consider the practical use of space; requirements for natural light and fresh air alongside those of privacy and warmth; color that sets the mood so that decor echoes function; furnishings gathered to reflect your taste; and the necessity for quiet in a noisy world.

Home comfort, however, is much more than the sum of these considerations. It is about contentment, health, well-being, and satisfaction in an atmosphere of domestic calm. It is the appreciation of something special, so subtle that it can hardly be defined. Many things contribute to home comfort: scented candles that bring a welcome glow to a cozy room, sizzling color to make you smile, sunshine and shade, and the reassuring passage of night to day. Most people would agree that comfort is at the heart of a home, yet for each of us, comfort is something different.

We all yearn for physical comfort: cushion-filled deep armchairs generous enough to accommodate children, too, and sofas to stretch out on at the end of the day. There is a sense of ease about familiar things – old wooden kitchen utensils and cooking

Ultimately, the greatest success of the house is that

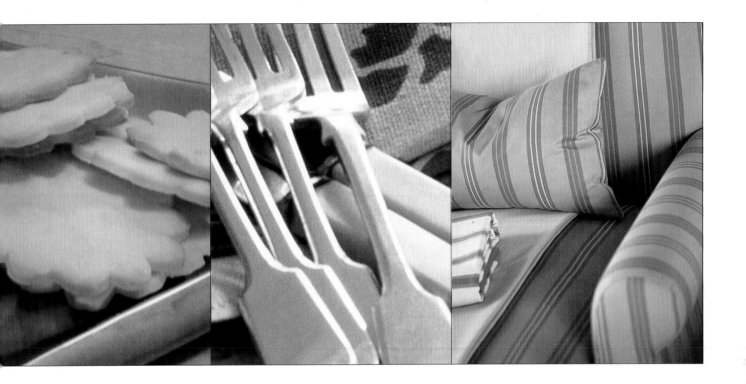

pots, polished floors, faded floral cloth, mismatched china – and in battered treasures rescued from flea markets. They share the character and allure of all time-worn things, and have dignity and an intrinsic beauty that transcends perfection. There is pleasure to be had, too, from what is recycled and inherited, objects that are chosen to last a lifetime, and those that are hand-crafted rather than mass-produced. Collections and sometimes whimsical mementos also enhance our feeling of comfort as heartening reminders of special people and places.

Even if occasionally it is carefully contrived, comfort must always seem effortless. The appeal of simple, practical living is its cornerstone, with reverence for what is truly useful (or truly loved), for comfort seems to evolve naturally from what is simple and sensible.

Whatever you do in your home, consider it in the light of comfort. Cooking, eating, bathing, sleeping: all the daily tasks are better done in comfort. Trust your instinct about the things you really value, and weed out what is unnecessary. Attune your home to how you live, and what you need it to be.

we can live ... comfortably and unselfconsciously.

Katie Asch, *Traditional Home®*

Relaxing

EVERYONE NEEDS a place to put up their feet or be quiet on their own, somewhere to escape the cares of the world. A weekend retreat is the ideal, but your refuge does not have to be so far removed from home. Hang up a *do not disturb* on a bedroom door or, if space is tight, use a folding screen to make a corner of a room private. In good weather, set a deck chair under a tree, or spread out a rug in the garden.

Take care to find some place in your home for the most welcome pastime of doing nothing at all.

WATCHING THE WORLD GO BY
Above Furniture that has seen better days will easily withstand a bit of weather. This sturdy, accommodating chair is positioned where its occupant can catch the sun, and can be pulled inside if rain threatens.

SUNSHINE & SHADE
Left Morning is the best time to enjoy the sun on this sheltered deck. Opening off of it, a comfortable, shady room is furnished with low tables and wing chairs dressed for the season in appropriately cool slipcovers.

SUMMERTIME & THE LIVING IS EASY
Right Transform a favorite garden spot or corner of a yard into your own place of peaceful repose by hanging a hammock between two trees or securing it to a wall with galvanized hooks and lengths of rope.

FIRESIDE GROUP WITH BOOKS
Left The fascinating display of graphic architectural prints in this elegant city apartment provides hours of enchanted contemplation and a marvelous talking point. Favorite books are all to hand, and a woven rug is an invitation to curl up before the fire on a winter evening.

MUSICAL INTERLUDE
Right An enjoyment of music is an important part of living well; making music yourself is even better. Wooden cladding insulates walls and prevents sound from traveling to other rooms, where silence may be appreciated.

Entertaining

CELEBRATIONS AND festivities were once the focus of family and social life, and entertaining at home satisfies a deep desire to gather together your closest family and friends. Whatever the season, welcome your guests in comfortable, relaxed surroundings, with sympathetic lighting to evoke an easy, lively atmosphere and suggest a holiday spirit. Show your warmth and consideration in small, thoughtful touches, and keep things simple to ensure that guests and hosts alike enjoy themselves.

Add thoughtful touches, such as posies of garden

COMPANIONABLE BREAKFAST
Above Even in a tiny apartment, there is a corner that will accommodate an intimate gathering. Here, chairs and a small table, generally used for writing letters, become the setting for a companionable breakfast and chat before the day's work begins.

INFORMAL DRINKS
Right Inviting friends for drinks at the end of a lazy summer day is entertaining at its simplest. Double doors thrown wide open allow this deck to become an extension of home for impromptu gatherings. Cheerful fabrics and casual furniture set the tone.

flowers, to make your guests feel really at home.

INVITATION TO THE BEACH
Left To enhance a natural setting, choose accessories with care. The soft pink of the oilcloth table cover looks delicious against the colors of sand and sea, and the cloth is cleverly weighted with pebbles found on the beach and tied to lengths of twine.

LUNCH IS SERVED
Right What better combination of colors could there be than the blues and yellows of this living-dining room? Soothing blue aids digestion and encourages rest after a good lunch, while spirited yellow ensures unflagging conversation during the meal.

Cooking & eating

SOME PEOPLE ARE inspired to make dishes to delight and bring them triumphantly to the table; for others, cooking is a chore. Like it or not, daily cooking requires patience, ingenuity with ingredients, and time, and the task will go more smoothly if your kitchen is a pleasing place to be as well as efficient. Preparing food and eating it in one room is convenient, and makes for happy interplay between diners and cook.

Homemade bread, pickles, and good cheese, eaten beside a cozy stove, are lovelier than any feast.

VISUAL INSPIRATION
Above A bowl of zingy citrus fruit and a rustic pottery flask of olive oil, with a stray sprig of delicate lady's mantle overhanging all, are enticing enough accoutrements to enthuse the most reluctant cook.

A TABLE FOR THREE, PLEASE
Left Rush-seated chairs and an old wooden table, reassuringly planted on sturdy square legs, create a dedicated eating place in this homey kitchen. Observe such comforting pieces as the terracotta utensil pots on the draining board and the oversized kettle.

THE HEART OF THE HOME
Right This narrow, tiny kitchen is equipped with all the essentials to cook and eat well. Open shelves display glassware and crocks in fine order, and a plumply cushioned sofa is the perfect spot to enjoy a quiet meal.

MOVABLE FEAST
Far left A neat round table, draped with a jolly checked cloth, has castors for ease of movement to another part of the kitchen. Here, it rests next to a counter-top electric griddle so that breakfasters need not wait for servings of pancakes and French toast.

SOCIABLE ARRANGEMENT
Left In a kitchen and dining room divided simply by wide, half-glazed doors – almost always left open – nothing comes between the cooks and those who have gathered at the table to enjoy the fruits of their labor.

Sleeping

WE SPEND much of our lives in bed, and restful sleep is important for good emotional and physical health. Bedrooms should therefore be as comfortable and peaceful as possible – cool, well-ventilated, and with clutter kept to a minimum. Heavy curtains help to absorb unwelcome noise from outside, although you may prefer to use a lighter fabric in warm weather. Try growing aloes in bedrooms since they refresh the air at night by replacing carbon dioxide with oxygen.

CANOPIED ELEGANCE
Above right A canopy of crocheted string is a practical embellishment for a four-poster bed in a hot climate, but any divan could be transformed into a romantic refuge by giving it the same treatment.

ROOM WITH BATH
Left Whites and creams are undemanding colors, custom-made for bedrooms. Here they set off the sculptural ironwork of the washstand and bedstead. Subtly patterned bedlinen echoes the checkered wood floor.

SYMMETRICAL SIMPLICITY
Right There is very little to disturb the eye in this bedroom of warm honey tones and white. Carefully balanced details add to its sense of calm, and the futon can be rolled and stored to liberate space, if necessary.

Crisply laundered linen with the

sweetness of flowers is an invitation to sleep late.

INNER SANCTUM
Left This restful room has a pleasing austerity that speaks of real luxury. Its spareness creates an uncluttered haven in which to unwind from the stresses of the day, and is not at all at odds with the comfort expected in a bedroom.

GUARDIAN ANGELS
Right Hours of repose and the sweetest of dreams are assured in a room that is filled with whimsical images of sleep: a man-in-the-moon bedhead, guardian angels and beasts, and a starry theme repeated in quiet hues above the bed.

Bathing

FOR MOST OF US, the ritual of bathing is special, and the bathroom is a haven for rejuvenation – a place to appreciate moments of solitude and enjoy the healing properties of water. Keep this naturally damp room fresh with good ventilation, letting moist air escape in exchange for dry. Insulate windows and doors, and raise the temperature when necessary. Cold air on bare skin is no joy on a frosty morning.

ON TOP OF THE WORLD
Above Set against azure sea and sky, a generously sized tin tub transforms an essential task into a grand experience.

BATHED IN GOLD
Far left Warm yellows and oranges are perfect for a cold bathroom. The wide edge of a pedestal sink holds toiletries in a room short on storage space.

WHITE METAL WITH GLASS
Left Fresh, clean, and light: white walls, chrome, aluminum, and glass bring a sense of space to any shower room.

Bathing outside is a modest way to free yourself from convention and the restrictions of daily life.

TIMELESS STYLE
Right Traditional fixtures complement a roll-top cast iron bath, which is fitted with a broad shelf on which treasures, necessities, and fragrant toiletries are kept safe and easily accessible.

PERFECTLY SIMPLE
Left An open-air bathroom is a fanciful notion, redolent of a sunny hideaway. Recreate a sense of tropical indolence in your bathroom with materials such as rubber wood, rush, and bamboo.

BATHROOM TO LINGER IN
Right Mirrors facing each other above washbasin and bath effectively widen a long, narrow bathroom. Mellow wood, soft colors, abundant daylight, books, and other comforts combine to make bathing here an everyday delight.

Working

THE NOTION of home as a place for leisure – a refuge after work – has perhaps always been more make-believe than real, for most homes are busy, productive places where there is always a floor to mop, a loaf of bread to bake, or household accounts to do. Whatever work you do at home, be it domestic, creative, or paid, create a space that will inspire your activity, and fill you with fresh energy and verve.

INSPIRING ATMOSPHERE
Above Charged with negative ions, sea air has a bracing quality that clears the mind and sharpens every sense. On a fine day, what more inspiring place to type a letter, start a book, or just appreciate the view?

CREATIVE USE OF SPACE
Right High-tech office equipment is often uncomfortable in a home setting; space at the top of the house is frequently unused. Make the best of both by turning a room under the eaves into an office, furnished with classic pieces that suit any decor.

CULTIVATING AN INTEREST
Left An amateur travel writer's workspace is crammed with the books, pictures, and artifacts that inform his craft. Looking at them is stimulating and a joy, so memories of travel are easily committed to paper.

BEDROOM ASIDE
Right A corner of your bedroom (or other room where people respect your privacy) can be set aside for you to work in peace. Place a table and chair where there is lots of light and air, and let the atmosphere of quiet repose fill you with brilliant plans.

DEDICATED WORKSPACE
Far right Designers' and artists' studios are good hunting grounds when seeking ideas for your own workspace. This pottery has abundant natural light, and the equipment is tailored to height and reach so that the potter can work tirelessly for long hours.

The tyranny of work becomes a pleasurable restraint when work is done in the comfort of home.

Taking it with you

THE WEARISOME ASPECT of travel is not eased by standardized hotels and boxy rented rooms. You can survive temporary lodgings and rise above their soullessness by decorating them with familiar things, with knick-knacks and creature comforts that make you feel at home. Take along photographs of loved ones; fill vases with fragrant flowers; and light scented candles for their gently calming or uplifting effect.

Wherever you go, the reassuring glow of lighted candles will work wonders to dispel old ghosts …

PORTABLE STORAGE
Above Knowing you have all the equipment you need on hand makes working in rented space much easier. Cube storage boxes can be transported from one place to another, and will hold anything from notepads and pens to files, framed prints, and mementos.

HEIRLOOM LINENS
Left Embroidered vintage voile bedcovers and fresh flowers make all the difference in the sparsely furnished attic bedroom of a holiday cottage, but if such linens are not to your taste, use a pretty shawl to double as a luxurious bedcover and evening wrap.

SIGNIFICANT COLOR
Right A rented apartment is much cheerier when brightened up with splashes of your favorite colors, as here on the cupboard doors. This inexpensive way to make your mark on a place is immensely satisfying.

FAMILY PHOTOGRAPHS & BOOKS
Far left Many seasoned travelers carry with them treasured items of sentimental value. The occupant of this modest country hotel room finds comfort in family photographs, displayed in pretty frames, and is lulled to sleep with well-thumbed paperbacks.

INEXPENSIVE EMBELLISHMENTS
Left You can personalize a plain – perhaps ill-equipped – kitchen in a vacation rental with inexpensive, useful accessories. Select items such as these matching jugs, wooden cutting boards, and jazzy dish towels, that will not look out of place at home.

Practical Resources

Materials for the projects in this book are widely available from hardware stores, arts and crafts suppliers, or department stores. These resources include general as well as specialist suppliers.

Accessories

Bed, Bath, and Beyond
800-462-3966
Accessories for the home, including linens and small appliances
Call for store locations

Crate and Barrel
888-249-4158
Home furnishings and equipment

Garnet Hill
231 Main Street
Franconia, NH 03580
800-622-6216
Accessories for the home in natural fibers and materials, including bedding and clothing
Call for catalogs (six annual catalogs also feature seasonal items)

J. Pocker & Son, Inc.
www.jpocker.com
Expert service in art and framing

Pier 1 Imports
800-477-4371
www.pier1.com
Furniture, lamps, candles, decorative accessories
Call for store locations

Pottery Barn
Mail Order Department
PO Box 7044
San Francisco, CA 94120-7044
800-922-5507
Phone and mail orders
Call for catalog and store locations

Arts and crafts materials

Dick Blick Art Materials
PO Box 1267
695 Route 150
Galesburg, IL 61402
309-343-6181
800-447-8192
www.dickblick.com
Arts and crafts supplies
Call for catalog and store locations

Candles, candle wax, and essential oils

Candleshtick
181 Seventh Avenue
New York, NY 10011
212-924-5444
Beeswax sheets in assorted colors

Green Lotus Aromatherapy
Company, Ltd.
14 Bruce Lane South
Kings Park, NY 11754
www.greenlotus.com
Paraffin wax, beeswax, essential oils

The Wax House
239 Market Street
Waynesboro, Virginia 22980
888-929-9711
www.waxhouse.com
Paraffin wax, beeswax, essential oils

Wicks n' Sticks
16825 Northchase Drive, Suite 900
Houston, TX 77060
281-874-0800; fax: 281-874-3678
www.wicksnsticks.com
Specialty candles and wax products
Call or check web page for store locations

Carpet and flooring

ABC Carpet & Home
888 Broadway
New York, NY 10003
212-473-3000

American Olean Tile Co.
1000 Cannon Avenue
Lansdale, PA 19446
215-855-1111
Ceramic tile
Call for ordering information

Kahrs Swedish Prefinished Wood Floors
800-784-8523
Call for product information and store locations

Embroidery threads

Connecting Threads
PO Box 8940
Vancouver, WA 98668
800-5745-6465
Discount fabric and sewing notions
Call for catalog

Clotilde, Inc.
10086 Sew Smart Way B8031
Stevens Point, WI 54481-8031
800-772-2891

Furniture and furnishings

Ballard Designs
800-284-5116
Call for catalog

IKEA
800-434-4532 (regional)
410-931-8940 (east coast)
818-912-1199 (west coast)
Call for catalog and store locations

Rowe Furniture
800-334-7693 ext. 800
www.rowefurniture.com
Call for store locations

Handles and fixtures

Kohler Co.
Kohler, Wisconsin 53044
800-456-4537
Bathroom faucets, handles, racks
Mail order available

Hardware and supplies

Home Depot
Corporate Offices
2727 Paces Ferry Road
Atlanta, GA 30339
800-553-3199
Lumber, fixtures, paint, wallpaper, carpet
Nationwide chain; call for catalog and store
locations

Lowe's Home Improvement Warehouses
Highway 268 East
North Wilkesboro, NC 28656
www.lowes.com
Lumber, fixtures, paint, wallpaper, flooring
Nationwide chain; check phone book for store
listings

Paint, pigments, and wall coverings

Benjamin Moore Paints
800-826-2623
888-236-6667
Call for store location and product information

Hunter-Douglas
2 Park Way South
Upper Straddle River, NJ 07458
800-327-2030
800-937-7895
Shades, blinds, vertical and horizontal dividers
Call for store locations

Kremer Pigments Inc.
228 Elizabeth Street
New York, NY 10012
212-219-2394

Pearl Paints
308 Canal Street
New York, NY 10013
800-221-6845
www.pearlpaint.com
email: Pearlsite@aol.com
Candle wicking and wick holder tabs by Walnut
Hill also available from this store

Storage

California Closets
Corporate Headquarters
1700 Montgomery Street
San Francisco, CA 94111
800-873-4264
800-325-6738
Custom closets
Call for brochure and store locations

The Container Store
2000 Valwood Parkway
Dallas, TX 75234-8880
800-733-3532
800-786-5858 (fax)
A complete line of storage items
Call for catalog and store locations

Hold Everything
3250 Van Ness Avenue
San Francisco, CA 91409
800-421-2264
Storage items designed to create space
Call for catalog and store locations

Rubbermaid
1147 Akron Road
Wooster, OH 44691
330-264-6464
Storage products for every room
Call for store locations

Index

Acknowledgments

Author's Acknowledgments

I can never thank Nicholas, Rose, Helena, and Margaret enough, for they have borne the brunt of my preoccupation with this book. Enormous thanks are due to my mother and father for their constant support, Charlie Beer, and my sister, Linda, who did not believe it would ever end. I am very grateful to James Merrell for the huge privilege of working with him, and to Nick Pope for unfailing good humor and great photographs. Thank you to Pam Donovan and Alice Taylor for patient, intricate stitching, Mike Donovan for fine woodwork, Liz Crouch, the best upholsterer I know, and Julian Cassell and Peter Parham, who gave decorative advice or help at a moment's notice and always make me smile. Keith, Victoria, Rufus, and Arthur Brooks are the best of friends who looked after me at the beginning and end of long London days; thank you. Needless to say, I could not have managed without the skill and experience of senior editor, Gillian Roberts, and project art editor, Clive Hayball, who steered me safely through the labyrinthine complexities of a DK book and made it fun too. I also thank Mollie Gillard, who searched tirelessly for the perfect picture, stylist Fanny Ward, who is an inspiration, and Wendy Bartlet, who took over the book design at a critical stage, and saw it through to the end. Many thanks to David Lamb for having faith in me, and to Anne-Marie Bulat for her vision. Finally, I would like to thank the companies who generously supplied materials for this book.

Publisher's Acknowledgments

Grateful thanks to the following people and companies for their essential contributions to *New Decorator*. Caroline Allen, Tom George, Denise O'Brien, Charlotte Oster, & Melanie Simmonds sourced pictures from the DK library; Hilary Bird compiled the index; Polly Boyd, Jane Cooke, & Lesley Malkin provided editorial assistance & encouraging comment; Robert Campbell helped prepare text film; Julian Cassell decorated the summerhouse pictured on pages 124–125, and restored it to its former state after it was photographed; Sonia Charbonnier answered the most trivial computer questions with willingness & a smile; Jemima Dyson provided an introduction to the location pictured on pages 124–125, and organized props from Laura Ashley; Sharon Moore & Alison Shackleton provided design assistance; Christine Murdock & Andrew Nash, Steve Knowlden & Ian Whitelaw helped to establish the concept for the book, and set the project photography in motion; Lyn Sherwood smoothed the way, and helped to organize the location pictured on pages 148–149; Mariana Sonnenberg assisted with picture research administration; Fanny Ward sourced props for the locations pictured on pages 46–47 & 124–125. Particular thanks to Margaret Howell, Laura Ashley, & Neal's Yard Remedies for providing props free of charge for the locations pictured on pages 124–125 & 148–149. Bill Mason & Dr Melville Roberts gave help, advice, & endless encouragement. Their contribution is greatly appreciated.

Location Photography

The publisher acknowledges the generous help of those who opened their homes for special photography. The Barnard Family, kitchen, pages 36–37, & living room, pages 44–45. Mr & Mrs John Dyson, summer-house, pages 124–125. Ellis Flyte, bedroom, page 4 third from top, dressing room, page 11 top right, party room, pages 46–47. Rebecca Hossack, bedroom, pages 70–71; Rebecca Hossack Gallery, 35 Windmill Street, London W1P 1HH, England, telephone 44 171 436 4899, specializes in Aboriginal art. Sue Macartney-Snape, studio flat, pages 156–157; designed by Jason Cooper Architects, 14 Alexander Street, London W2 5NT, England, telephone 44 171 727 3104; thanks also to Dominic Best, who was renting the apartment. Mr & Mrs Ian Mankin, bathroom, pages 148–149. Thanks also to those whose homes were considered but not photographed: Chris & Julia Cowper, Mr & Mrs Etienne Milner, Henrietta Petit, Julia Pashley, Mary Wondrausch.

Commissioned Photography

Step-by-step projects by James Merrell & Nick Pope, who was assisted by Lee Hind & (on one occasion) Giles Westley. Locations (as detailed above) by Nick Pope, assisted by Lee Hind. Other photography by Peter Anderson, Tim Ridley, Matthew Ward.

Illustrations

Murdo Culver, Richard Lee.

Agency picture credits appear on page 192.

Agency Picture Credits

The publisher would like to thank the following sources for their kind permission to reproduce their photographs in this book.

t: top, b: below, l: left, r: right, c: center

Abode: Ian Parry 93tr, 158bl, 165br, 175tl, 180cl; **Trevor Richards** 82–83bc. **Arcaid: Richard Bryant** 164bl, **/Designer Peter Leonard** 22–23b; **Mark Burgin/Belle** 130–131, 146–147b; **Earl Carter/Belle** 99c, 100–101c; **David Churchill** 146bc; **Annet Held** 176bl; **Simon Kenny/Belle** 8tl, 76–77b; **Geoff Lung/Belle** 23tr; **Alberto Piavano** 110–111; **Alan Weintraub** 9r, 110br, 115tr, 159br, 164br, 170tr, 172cla, 172br, 177, 179bl, 183bc. **Laura Ashley:** 4bl, 5crb, 105tc, 162–163, 172tr. **Anthony Blake Photo Library:** 138tl. **Country Living: James Merrell** 72bl, 87br. **Bruce Coleman Ltd: Kim Taylor** 154tc. **Design Press/ Lars Hallen:** 16tl, 16tr, 92bl, 146tr. **Designers Guild:** 3cr, 66tl, 104tl, 106tc, 170tl, 171tr. **Fired Earth:** 2cr, 133tr. **Richard Glover:** 8–9b, **/John Pawson** 40–41. **Habitat:** 42tl. **Robert Harding Syndication: John Miller** 12–13c, **Brian Harrison** 184cl; **Brad Simmons** 12t; **IPC Magazines Ltd/Country Homes & Interiors: Simon Brown** 138bl, **Leim Sayer** 126bl, **Fritz von der Schulenburg** 147tc; **Homes & Gardens: Jan Baldwin** 86–87c, 136tr, 184bl; **Andreas von Einsiedel** 126–127br; **Ken Kirkwood** 175br; **Tom Leighton** 174c; **Mark**

Luscombe-Whyte 18br; **John Mason** 178c; **Jonathan Pilkington** 171tl; **Simon Upton** 98br, 100tl, 108tr, 134–135b; **Pia Tryde** 180tr; **Homes & Ideas: Spike Powell** 85tr; **Ideal Home: Mark Luscombe-White** 84b; **Options: James Merrell** 173c, 175cr, 183tl; **Wedding & Home: Tom Leighton** 184bc. **The Holding Company:** 118–119c. **Houses & Interiors: Roger Brookes** 60–61b, 79bl, 183cr; **Simon Butcher** 90bl; **Verne** 114cb, 142–143, 183br. **Ikea Ltd/ Condor Public Relations:** 20–21cb. **The Interior Archive: Tim Beddow** 22–23t, 51br, 82–83t, 135tl, 176cla; **Simon Brown** 32tl, **/R. Banks Pye** 32–33; **Mimmi O'Connell** 54–55; **J. Pilkington** 179cr; **Fritz von der Schulenburg** 9br, 19, 72–73, 78bl, 98bl, 104–103tl, 114tl, 122–123c, 138–139, 179tr, 179br, 180br, 180bl; **C. Simon Sykes** 5tl, 64–65, 92–93, 104bc, 146tl, 159bl; **Simon Upton** 182; **Henry Wilson** 50tl; **Wayne Vincent** 18tl; **Peter Woloszynski** 26–27, 87tr.

Paul Ryan/International Interiors: /Designer Kathy Gallagher 158tl, **/Ina Garten** 30–31b, **/Designer Christian Liaigre** 51bl, **/Designer Jo Nahem** 86bl, **/Designer Kristina Ratia** 85bc, 123bl, **/Designers D & V Tsingaris** 31bc. **Ray Main/Mainstream Photography:** 4t, 14–15, 20bl, 21br, 22tl, 50bc, 60bc, 68br, 69br, 72bc, 76tr, 78br, 78–79t, 79br, 93br, 96–97c, 101tr, 106–107, 123br, 127r, 134tr, 152–153, 180c, 184tr, 185c 83br, **/Cinnalil Islington** 110tl. **Simon McBride:** 6–7, 134tl. **James Merrell/Nicholas Barnard:** 5bl, 6bl, 18bl, 126tl, 126–127t, 172bl, 181. **Tim Street-Porter: /Designer Michael Anderson** 122tl, **/Designer Chuck Arnold** 101br, **/Designer Paul Fortune** 56–57, **/Designer Myra Hoefer** 32bl, **/Designer Philippe Starck** 3cl, 60tl. **Telegraph Colour Library: /Japack Photo Library** 170tc. **View: Phillip Bier** 168–169; **Peter Cook:** front cover, 30bl, 56bl, 57br, 60–61t, 159t, **/Simon Cander Associates** 77r; **/Nico Rench** 23tc, **/Troughton McAslan** 30–31t, 114–115, **/Designer Tugman Partnership** 20–21bl, **/Designer Michael Winter** 50–51t; **Dennis Gilbert:** 10, **/Sanya Polescuk** 110bl, 115br. **Elizabeth Whiting & Associates:** 105tr; **Michael Dunne** 164–165tr; **Andreas von Einsiedel** 91br, 122bl; **Brian Harrison** 33tr; **Tom Leighton** 5br, 176tr; **Mark Luscombe-Whyte** 90–91tc; **Spike Powell** 82tl, 84tl, 90–91bc; **Dennis Stone** 84–85tc, 139br; **Peter Woloszynski** 165bc.